THE PINKEST PARTY ON EARTH

To: Nancy

Have fun at the party!

Ed Guscino

MERCER
UNIVERSITY PRESS

Endowed by
TOM WATSON BROWN
and
THE WATSON-BROWN FOUNDATION, INC.

THE
PINKEST
PARTY ON EARTH

Macon, Georgia's
International Cherry Blossom Festival

ED GRISAMORE

Mercer University Press | Macon, Georgia

MUP/P482

© 2014 Mercer University Press
1400 Coleman Avenue
Macon, Georgia 31207
All rights reserved

First Edition

Book design by Burt&Burt

ISBN 978-0-88146-480-1

Cataloging-in-Publication Data is available from the Library of Congress

TABLE OF CONTENTS

David Fowlkes, left, a member of the AmStar Cinemas team, won the festival's first annual high heel race in 2011 wearing 2-inch heels. (Photo by Beau Cabell)

WELCOME TO THE PARTY

It begins with the arrival of pink wreaths on doors and pink bows on mailboxes.

Pink poodles, carved out of wood, begin appearing on neighborhood lawns. Not even the city's leash law can stop 'em.

Suddenly, storefronts and windshields are displaying painted petals. Pink becomes the official enamel for everything.

Folks sink their forks into pink pancakes and gather for free pink ice cream at the park. They nibble on pink cornbread at downtown restaurants. Even *The Telegraph*, the city's newspaper since 1826, is delivered with the morning news splashed across pink paper on the first day of the Cherry Blossom Festival in Macon, Georgia.

There is so much pink that folks have to rub their eyes. For ten days, Macon becomes a "tint" city.

Welcome to the Pinkest Party on Earth.

The Yoshino cherry trees are, of course, the stars of the show. Festival officials place their number at more than 300,000. This translates into three trees for every man, woman, and child in the city. Half the dogs and dog-woods, too.

In the archives of the Congressional Record in Washington, DC—a city also known for its rich Yoshino hue—Macon is cited as the "Cherry Blossom Capital of the World."

Dan Reusch and his wife, Beth, of Peoria, Ill., fire up their balloon at the 2011 festival. (Photo by Beau Cabell)

Spring is Macon's shining armor. When the sky is blue, the air is warm, and the city is in full bloom, there is no prettier place on earth. The Cherry Blossom Festival is Macon's chance to let down its hair, strut its stuff, and flirt with the world. It's a time when the community puts aside its differences and divisiveness, its emotions and territorial rights. It doesn't matter if someone is rich or poor, black or white, Republican or Democrat. There's a unified front, tied together with a pink ribbon, to share in the beauty and pageantry.

It's not March Madness. It's March Gladness.

"It is the one event every year that brings Macon together," said Reverend Ronald Terry, pastor at New Fellowship Missionary Baptist and a longtime festival board member. "All over the world, people look at Macon as the cherry blossom capital. It's a great opportunity for us to show off our city."

The festival makes folks in Macon so proud to live here that their buttons are popping off all those pink shirts. It makes them want to shout— or maybe wear a huge sign around their necks—to let everyone know that this is their hometown. They walk around with an extra bounce in their step. It's called pride in owner-ship.

Connie Howard gets the festival gift shop ready in 2009. (Photo by Beau Cabell)

Tourists roll into town with out-of-state license plates to gush over the blossoms. They are drawn to Macon from all over, as if the blossoms had a curious force inside their petals. Visitors peer out windows of tour buses, marveling at the city's rich history, incredible architectural beauty, and huge helpings of Southern hospitality.

The festival has been lauded for its ability to provide something for everyone and everything for some. It gets high marks for its inclusiveness. There are cultural oppor-tunities, educational programs, music, food, sports, shopping, worship services, architectural and history lessons, and horticultural beauty.

Some folks love the parade; others have never missed a balloon glow. There are bed races, concerts, golf tournaments, garden tours, street parties, fireworks, and, of course, free cherry ice cream.

Most of the events are free, too, thanks to the generosity of corporate sponsors and the tireless dedication of hundreds of volunteers.

Step right up to the pinkest show on earth. It's party time.

William A. Fickling Sr. became known as "Johnny Cherryseed" in the community. (Photo by Beau Cabell)

JOHNNY CHERRYSEED

His name rises in big red letters at the top of a fifteen-story office building, the tallest in the city, at the corner of Second and Mulberry.

The driveway to the house where he lived on Ingleside Avenue, as wide as a four-lane at the bottom, is a major tourist attraction every March. Cars, buses, and television crews from ABC's *Good Morning America* have pulled in to admire the cherry trees.

It's like a postcard, and visitors strike poses for photographs because they could never go home and attempt to describe this beauty in words. This is where it all began, the Bethlehem of the blossoms and the birthplace of the pinkest party on earth.

The name of William Arthur Fickling, Sr., has been passed down to his son, grandson, and great-grandson.

But to all who know his story, he was affectionately known as "Johnny Cherryseed."

The flowering cherry trees are his legacy. A generous man, he gave away more than 120,000 trees in his lifetime to the community he dearly loved. Most of the city's more than 300,000 Yoshinos come from some branch of the Fickling family trees and Macon leads the Free World in cherry blossoms.

Perhaps no other man in the twentieth century contributed more to the growth and development of Macon than Bill Fickling, Sr. He was a father figure to the community.

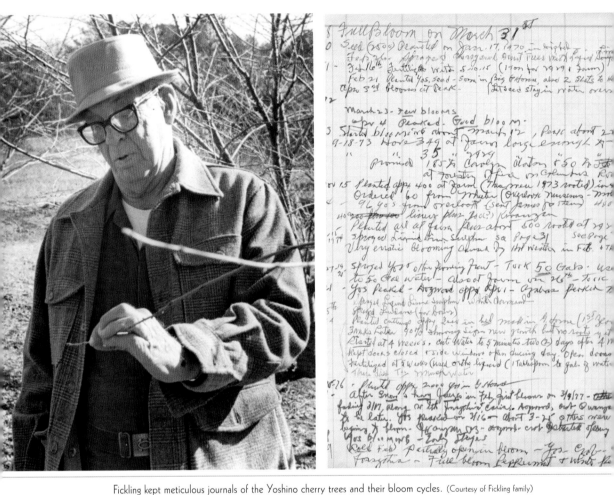

Fickling kept meticulous journals of the Yoshino cherry trees and their bloom cycles. (Courtesy of Fickling family)

When Fickling died in 1990 at age eighty-seven, former mayor Tommy Olmstead spoke of Fickling's legacy. "In every generation, there is one person who can be a catalyst and cause great things to happen," said Olmstead. "In my generation, that man was William Fickling."

Fickling built a multi-million-dollar real estate and insurance empire. He was one of Macon's most beloved leaders, philanthropists, and civic-minded citizens. He was involved in almost every way in the heartbeat of the city—from the Chamber of Commerce to the industrial authority to planning and zoning. He served on the school board during integration and, although he was white, was involved with the local chapter of the NAACP.

Known for his honesty and fairness in dealing with people, he held only one political office, serving on the county commission from 1953 to 1957. He never made a single speech or purchased a single campaign ad during the election. He simply wrote letters to registered voters and told them he would appreciate their support.

He was instrumental in Interstate 75 coming through Macon after the original plans in 1955 called for it to bypass the city like Sherman on his march to the beach. He was a devoted member of Mulberry Street United Methodist Church. He was owner of the Macon Peaches minor league baseball team. He was one of the original owners of Riverside Ford. He also possessed a different kind of horsepower. In 1960, he owned a world champion horse, a Tennessee Walker named Mack K's Handshaker.

But he is most remembered for the cherry trees.

Fickling's deep roots run back to Reynolds, Georgia, where he was born on March 23, 1903. He was the only child of Dr. George Walker Fickling and Lucy Wilson Fickling. His father was a dentist in Reynolds, and the family lived on Main Street. He worked and played at his grandfather's grist mill, Fickling Mill, in Taylor County.

His ancestors made their marks on history. Major Benjamin Franklin Ficklin, who carried a different spelling of his last name, founded the Pony Express. He also established stagecoach and mail routes in the West and founded the Pacific Telegraph Company. Orlando Bell Ficklin, a congressman from Illinois, was selected to moderate the famous Lincoln-Douglas debates in 1858. Eldred Simkins Fickling was a captain and the tallest soldier (at 6 feet, 9 inches) in the Confederate Army.

Fickling was an outstanding student at Reynolds High School, where he graduated in 1919. He excelled in math. He could look at a column of numbers and quickly add them in his head. His parents sent him to Emory at Oxford, and his mother wanted

Fickling as a young man.
(Courtesy of Fickling family)

him to study to be a doctor. But math was his passion, not medicine, and he returned home after college to teach math at the high school.

Fickling was tall and athletic, a good baseball player in his younger days. His big feet—he wore a size eleven shoe when he was twelve years old—earned him the nickname "Foots." He had strong hands, too.

Those hands also sported a pair of green thumbs. He got them from his mother. Lucy Fickling was an avid gardener. She loved roses and grew herbs, rooting flowers and plants in glass jars. Her son grew up playing in the dirt.

"I like to share my mother's love of flowers," Fickling once said in an interview. "I was brought up to love them. People would stop by our house to buy cuttings of my mother's flowers, but she would not sell them. She would give them away."

Later in life, Fickling never put a price tag on his cherry trees. They were an extraordinary gift, and he was the humble giver.

He met his wife, Claudia Foster Fickling, when he quit teaching and went to look for work in Macon at age twenty-four. She was originally from Kentucky, and she came to Macon to live with her aunt on Foster Road.

Fickling was hired by Washington Dessau Realty in Macon and assigned as a rent collector in some of the city's poorest neighborhoods, including sections of the black community.

"Seeing the conditions that existed in these neighborhoods was to make a lifelong impression on him," said his grandson, Bill Fickling III. "Years later, he quietly supported the civil rights movement. Empathy for the plight of others and quiet devotion to his chosen causes were characteristics that stayed with him for his entire life."

Fickling and Claudia married in 1927 and had two children, William Arthur Fickling, Jr., and the late Virginia Monfort. (They had seven grandchildren: Bill Fickling III, Jane Dru Skinner, Julia Tiller, Roy Fickling, Kathy Wright, Virginia Rabun, and William Monfort Jr.)

The elder Fickling quit Dessau after twelve years to strike out on his own. He borrowed $300 from his mother to start his own real estate company, and he struggled through the first couple of years. In 1939, he formed a team with B. Sanders Walker, who sold insurance. While having lunch at a downtown restaurant one day, Fickling lamented the ups and downs of real estate. When things went well, they went really well. But when things went poorly, there was barely enough income to provide for his family. Walker, meanwhile, talked about the relative stability of selling insurance. He might not be able to make big money, but at least there would always be a steady paycheck.

The two men formed Fickling and Walker, using the money they made from insurance to pay the bills and the income from real estate to reach for the stars.

Walker and Fickling were in the right place at the right time. They helped negotiate the land deals to build Brosnan Yard, a major switching station for Southern Railroad. Their business fortunes soared during World War II, when the sleepy little train depot of Wellston became Warner Robins, now the seventh largest city in Georgia. It was home to Robins Air Field, which became Robins Air Force Base and is now the largest civilian employer in Georgia.

"My grandfather would tell stories about developing streets and homes in Warner Robins," said Bill III. "He would drive down there and have a sale on Saturday afternoons. He would have a stack of twenty contracts with him, and people would line up. That's how fast they were selling houses."

Fickling began developing neighborhoods not only in Macon and Warner Robins but also across the state and region. He built shopping centers in Atlanta and apartment and housing units in Florida. In 1961, he developed Westgate Mall, the first enclosed mall in Georgia, on property that was once a dairy farm.

Left, Fickling and great-grandson John Wright, 3, share birthday cake at Third Street Park in 1987. (Photo by Beau Cabell)
Right, Fickling at his farm on Rivoli. (Courtesy of Fickling family)

He had experience with dairies. In 1948, he had built his own home on what was once the old Bowman Dairy Farm in Macon. It was part of a neighborhood he called Brookwood Hills. Back then, the residential side of Ingleside Avenue was a dirt road and outside the city limits.

Fickling home at 2929 Ingleside as it looked in the early 1950s. (Courtesy of Fickling family)

He sold almost every lot before claiming his own. The property at 2929 Ingleside Avenue didn't have the best curb appeal. He purchased 6 acres on a steep hill with Bowman Creek running through the bottom.

"It didn't look anything like it does today," said Bill III, who now lives with his family in the home his grandfather made famous. "It had been clear-cut because it was a dairy farm. It was just an ugly dirt hill with a few trees on it. At the time, most people wanted flat lots and wouldn't build on any kind of slope at all. He took the leftover property."

Fickling may have been a real estate giant, but he was the jolly green gardener at heart. He went to work with plans to landscape his yard and hired a local nursery to help him beautify the property.

The original plans called for dogwoods, one of the most popular trees in the South, to be planted across the steep slope of the front yard. He even had cards printed that read, "Dogwoods and Southern Charm."

When several trees bloomed the following spring, right around his March 23 birthday, Fickling was charmed by their beauty.

Upon closer examination, though, he realized they were not dogwoods. And there had been no identification tags on the trees.

"He went back to the nursery and asked what they were," said Bill III. "The landscape plan said dogwoods, and he was expecting them. Somehow, through fate, providence, or whatever, they got switched out. The Yoshinos were planted by accident."

The nursery owner apologized but could not identify the trees, either. Yoshino cherry trees were foreign to most South Georgia nurseries. The trees are more favorable to colder climates and are prone to insect borers commonly found in the South.

Fickling didn't play much golf or fish, and he didn't take vacations to exotic places. His passion was working in his yard. He had a greenhouse on the back of his property. Over the years, he grew prize camellias. So he was no dummy when it came to horticulture. But the mystery trees had him—pardon the pun—stumped.

His friends and neighbors would stop by to admire them and ask where they could get one. Fickling would just shrug.

"I don't even know what it is," he told them.

That did not stop him from trying to make the trees multiply. Because there were no seeds, he began experimenting with ways to propagate them in his greenhouse. Whenever someone was curious, he would hand the person a pot with a small tree that he had successfully rooted.

Longtime friend Ed Sell, a local attorney, used to claim that "you could always tell who Bill Fickling's friends were because they all had one of those unusual trees in their yards."

Founder's Day is traditionally held on March 23 to honor Fickling's memory with a cake on his birthday. (Photo by Jay Jarvis)

It took three years for Fickling to learn the identity of the trees. He had friends in high places, including US Representative Carl Vinson, and made frequent trips to Washington to bend his ear.

On a spring visit in 1952, he noticed the beautiful Yoshino trees in DC and marveled at their resemblance to the ones in his yard at home. He was convinced that they had some kinfolks back in Macon. So he snipped a small branch, packed the cutting on ice, and headed home for a reunion.

(The year 1952 brought another kind of beauty into the lives of the Fickling family. The lovely Neva Jane Langley won the title of Miss Wesleyan, Miss Macon, and Miss Georgia in fall 1952 and wore the crown of Miss America 1953. She married Fickling's son, Bill, Jr,. two years later.)

Historic marker for Fickling "Father of Cherry Blossoms" in Third Street Park. (Courtesy of Cherry Blossom Festival)

Fickling labored until he found the correct combinations of sun, soil, and moisture. He had some successes and plenty of failures. But, like Thomas Edison with the light bulb, he did not give up.

He began contacting nurseries in northern states. When he spoke to someone at the National Arboretum, he learned Yoshinos do not prosper in the heat, so the greenhouse was a less-than-ideal place.

His front yard, however, provided an almost perfect ecosystem. When the yard was landscaped, sandy topsoil was brought up from the Ocmulgee River. Yoshinos do best when planted on a slope, with proper drainage, and in the shade of coniferous trees, like the pine trees that stood guard near the front of the house. (The irony now is had Fickling selected a flat, muddy lot to build his house, those trees might never have survived.)

For more than a decade, he rooted some 15,000 cuttings a year at his 140-acre farm on Rivoli Drive. He hired a man from Reynolds, Arthur Childree, to be the caretaker on the property. And Childree, now in his nineties, helped turn the Rivoli property into a showcase for the trees.

Fickling experimented with dozens of varieties of other ornamental cherries, including Kwanzan and shidarezakura (weeping cherry). He kept meticulous journals of the trees and their bloom cycles.

He also continued to give the trees away to anyone who asked. His wife, Claudia, kept a year-round request list. They were given to garden clubs and civic groups. They were planted in schoolyards and at churches, retirement homes, hospitals, parks, and college campuses. Fickling's grandchildren gave them to their teachers.

"They are so beautiful they just give themselves away," he once said. "I only help pot them up."

In 1973, Fickling held a picnic at his farm. Among the guests was Carolyn Crayton.

She told Fickling she had a dream of planting cherry trees all over the city. It was her vision to have them in neighborhoods and parks, a Yoshino on every corner. She wanted to know if he would help her make that happen.

It was the beginning of a beautiful friendship.

The front yard of the Fickling home on Ingleside is the "Bethlehem of Blossoms" and birthplace of the "Pinkest Party on Earth" (Photo by Beau Cabell)

THE FAMILY TREE

A perfect cherry blossom is a rare thing.
You can spend your whole life looking for one,
and it will not be a wasted life.
—*from* The Last Samurai

The granddaddy tree still lives on the slope of the hill, steeped in history, dirt, grass, and ivy.

It stands guard at the stately, white-columned house at 2929 Ingleside Avenue, built by William Fickling, Sr., in the late 1940s.

Its brothers have gone on to that great woodpile in the sky. It is the last man standing of those mystery trees that filled gaps in the Fickling yard with no thoughts of ever becoming legendary.

The surviving senior citizen has been chipped and chiseled by the years, and some say it lives on borrowed time. The life expectancy of a Yoshino in the South is thirty to forty years, so this tree is well settled into its golden years.

It has spread its roots into the sandy topsoil brought from the river. The hillside provides good drainage, and the pine trees offer just the right amount of shade. The tree has endured hot Georgia summers, ice storms, high winds, and wood-boring insects.

Bill Fickling III with "granddaddy tree" in 2001 with sons Dru, 12, and William IV, 11. (Photo by Beau Cabell)

"It was planted in the ideal spot, even though my grandfather might not have known it at the time," said Bill Fickling III, who now lives in the house. "It was serendipity. Of course, it has all been serendipity."

Bill keeps a photograph of the old home place that was taken the year his grandfather built the house a few years after the end of World War II. The infant Yoshino tree is visible in the picture. It was not much taller than his dad, Bill Jr., who was a 6-foot-4 basketball player at Lanier High School and Auburn University.

The tree now has two generations of rings around its belly and is more than 30 feet tall. The original base is a plump 7 feet in diameter. (Including an offshoot, the base is 12 feet.)

Bill estimates some 95 percent of Macon's more than 300,000 cherry trees have come from the cuttings, grafts, and propagation of those pioneer Yoshinos.

That's a large family tree.

Of course, the roots have spread across the more than 7,200 miles to Mount Yoshino in Japan. They are part of a genus of more than 400 species of the non-fruit-bearing trees with the botanical name prunus x yedoensis.

The origin of the trees can be traced back for centuries, as far back as AD 812, when Emperor Saga gave the first hanami (cherry blossom viewing party) at the Imperial Palace in Kyoto.

The Yoshino is the most popular of the more than 200 varieties of flowering cherry trees in Japan. The blossoms represent springtime and love and are considered symbols of good fortune. The cherry blossom emblem can be found on the back of a 100-yen coin (about $1).

The trees were first planted in Washington, DC, in 1912 as a gift of friendship and love from Japan.

The idea to plant cherry trees along the Potomac came in 1885. Eliza Scidmore was a newspaper correspondent and the first female board member of the National Geographic Society. She was an authority on Asian culture and had returned from a trip to Japan. There was lukewarm support for her proposal. She may have been discouraged, but she refused to give up.

In 1906, David Fairchild, a prominent figure at the US Department of Agriculture, ordered 100 flowering cherry trees from a nursery in Japan. He planted them at his home in Chevy Chase, Maryland, and soon began to advance the idea of lining the avenues in Washington with the beautiful trees. He gave saplings to schools in the District of Columbia and encouraged them to plant the trees in observance of Arbor Day. He joined Scidmore in campaigning for a "Field of Cherries" around the Tidal Basin.

Scidmore began looking for ways to raise money to donate the cherry trees to the city. In 1909, she found an ally after writing a letter to First Lady Helen "Nellie" Taft. It was not a hard sell, since Taft was familiar with the cherry trees. President William Howard Taft had been appointed by President William McKinley to serve as governor of the newly acquired Philippine Islands following the Spanish-American War. She was inspired by how the cherry blossoms in Manila's Luneta Park brought people of all classes together to admire their beauty. She wanted the same for the nation's capital.

Taft accepted a donation of 2,000 trees from the Japanese consul, and they arrived in Washington in January 1910. But inspectors with the US Department of Agriculture discovered the trees were infected with insects and nematodes and ordered them destroyed to protect native trees. They were later burned.

Japanese officials expressed regret over the diseased trees and, in a gesture of goodwill, sent 3,020 trees on February 14, 1912, which was, appropriately enough, Valentine's Day. The delivery included twelve varieties from scions of the famed trees along the Arakawa River in Tokyo.

First Lady Taft and Viscountess Chinda, the wife of the Japanese ambassador, had a ceremonial planting of the first two trees on March 27, 1912, on the northern bank of the Tidal Basin. (In return, First Lady Taft presented Viscountess Chinda with a bouquet of roses.) The remaining trees were planted over the next eight years, including on the grounds at the White House. The city of Washington held the first "National Cherry Blossom Festival" in 1935.

Over the years, the trees had to endure more than bad weather and insect infestations. In what was known as the "Cherry Tree Rebellion" in 1938, a group of prominent Washington society women chained themselves to the trees to protest the removal of many of the trees to begin construction of the new Jefferson Memorial.

Also, some of the trees were vandalized following Japan's attack on Pearl Harbor in December 1941, which led to America's entry into World War II. The strain in relations between the two countries was resolved following the war, and cuttings from trees growing along the Tidal Basin were sent to Japan to help replenish the groves of cherry trees that were destroyed during the bombings of Hiroshima and Nagasaki.

Seven years after the war, on a trip to Washington, DC, William Fickling, Sr., clipped a small branch from one of the trees around the Tidal Basin and compared it to his own.

Arthur Childree at Fickling Farm in 2010. (Photo by Beau Cabell)

Back home, he continued to give away cherry trees almost as fast as he could grow them.

One tree begat another. And another. And another.

The man who helped him was Arthur Childree.

By the time Childree arrived into the world, Fickling was eighteen years old and had left his home in Reynolds to attend college. About the only real association Childree had with the Fickling family was that Dr. Fickling, the town dentist, had once pulled a few of Childree's teeth.

On a spring day in 1957, Childree knocked on the door of the Fickling home in Reynolds and told Lucy he was looking for work. She suggested he apply for a job at her son's office in Macon the next morning.

She told him it was across from the courthouse. Just ask anybody, she said, and they could tell him where it was.

Childree was up with the rooster and arrived at Fickling's office before 8:00 a.m. Fickling hired him as caretaker for the 140-acre farm on Rivoli. Childree's duties were to keep the grass cut and the fences mended and to look after the Hereford cattle. He moved to the farm with his wife, Ruby, on April 16, 1957, his thirty-sixth birthday.

At the home on Ingleside, Fickling raised his trees like children, caring for them and nurturing them. And Childree was always at his side. They became like brothers. If Fickling was the admiral of the *S.S. Yoshino*, then Childree was his first mate.

"He would come home for lunch every day, and we would work in the greenhouses," said Childree. "I didn't know anything about the cherry trees when I started. But I learned."

Fickling would take clippings 6 inches long, strip off the leaves except at the top, and then dip them in water to root them. He would later stick them in soil about half the length of a man's finger. Childree learned the process too, as if by osmosis.

In the years that followed, Fickling began giving away more trees, usually when they reached a height of 5 feet. His supply could hardly keep up with demand. He began purchasing the trees from several different nurseries in the Southeast.

Childree would drive to Alabama, and later to Tennessee, bringing back thousands of cherry trees. He would fill the spacious pasture at the farm with as many as 15,000 at a time, digging holes with a backhoe and clearing the fields with a tractor. When the rows became too narrow, he would use a mule to plow the tight spots.

Fickling took pride in the picture-postcard beauty of the farm. He also took satisfaction in the Fickling yard at Ingleside, which became a showcase the third week of March every spring.

People would stop to admire the blossoms.

On a spring day in March 1970, a family from Chattanooga, Tennessee, came to Macon for a visit. The man was a textile engineer and had been offered a job at the Bibb Company. He brought his wife and two children, who had never been to Macon.

The family toured the neighborhoods in midtown and north Macon. As they rounded the curve on Ingleside Avenue, at the bottom of the hill, the Fickling's yard came into view. The cherry trees were in full bloom.

Lee Crayton turned to his wife, Carolyn, and said, "I believe this is meant to be."

Carolyn Crayton, godmother of the "Pinkest Party," outside festival headquarters on Cherry Street in 2000. (Photo by Beau Cabell)

FIRST LADY OF PINK

The invitation to what would become the pinkest party on earth was issued in the spring of 1970.

Lee and Carolyn Crayton were living in their dream home north of Chattanooga on Signal Mountain. They had stone dug out of Cumberland Mountain to build their house on North Palisades Drive. On a clear day, they could look out their window and see the tops of five states.

Lee was a highly sought-after executive in the textile industry. He had a great job with Dixie Yarns. Nobody thought he would leave. Of course, nobody thought he would ever leave his native North Carolina, either.

But an old friend, Will Manning, was president of the Bibb Company in Macon. He kept calling. And every time Manning came back with another offer, Lee respectfully declined.

Lee Crayton and Carolyn Mullis had grown up four blocks from each other in Concord, North Carolina. Their parents worked in the mills. Lee was quiet and studious. He was valedictorian at Concord High School and finished with the highest grades in his class at North Carolina State.

Carolyn was raised in a home with three older brothers and a sister. She sang in the church choir. One Sunday, she looked out and saw a handsome young man in the congregation. She knew his mother and father, but she had never noticed him before.

One day, he noticed her, too. She walked by his home on the way to visit her grandmother, stopping to talk to him in the yard. When it started getting late, she told him she didn't want her grandmother to worry. He insisted on giving her a ride in his car.

"Why don't we stop by the creamery and get ice cream?" he suggested.

It was a good day for ice cream.

They continued to date, even after he went off to NC State to study textile engineering. Carolyn broke her back playing basketball her junior year of high school. Doctors took a bone from her leg and fused it to her spine so she could walk again. She spent months in a body cast.

They married two days before Christmas in 1948 and moved to Greensboro, North Carolina, where Carolyn became involved in civic activities and community service. She started the Greensboro Beautiful Commission and initiated a plan in the 1960s to plant roses along the stretch of I-40 that passed through the city.

It was her work with area high school students that brought recognition of her efforts to a larger platform. After some local teenagers had done extensive damage to a hotel following a dance, the school superintendent asked for Carolyn's help in channeling some of the teens' destructive energy into a constructive project.

She challenged the city's five high schools in a contest to clean up and landscape their campuses. She convinced athletes, cheerleaders, and other popular students to get involved, and her idea took off from there. She remembers how students at one of the schools grouped their cars in a circle so they could use the headlights to complete a landscape project at night.

Carolyn began getting requests from other communities to share information about her program. At a conference in Jackson, Mississippi, reporters from *Southern Living* were in the audience.

"When I finished speaking," she said, "they came up and said, 'I hope you don't mind, but we're going home with you.' They spent a week in Greensboro. When the story came out, the chamber of commerce had to help me with all the phone calls."

When the Craytons moved to Chattanooga, Carolyn was appointed to the Scenic City Commission. The two of them were happy. They thought they would settle in Chattanooga with their children, Annette and Doug.

About the only thing Lee and Carolyn had in common with Macon was that the city was named after Nathaniel Macon, a well-known nineteenth-century statesman from their native North Carolina.

Company officials bent Lee's ear and tugged on his heart. In March 1970, he drove Carolyn and the children to Macon to visit the city for the first time. They arrived on a newly opened stretch of I-75 and got off at the Riverside Drive exit. Lee glanced over at the fence along the interstate and told Carolyn it looked like a perfect place to plant roses, just as she did in Greensboro.

And then the cherry trees sealed the deal. The Craytons were riding around exploring neighborhoods, and they drove down Ingleside Avenue. The Yoshinos were blooming. It was as if Macon had rolled out a pink welcome mat.

They bought a lot on Guerry Drive and began building the fifth house in the new Wesleyan Woods subdivision. Developer Wallace Rivers helped them select the property. They had traded a mountain in Chattanooga for a slope in north Macon.

Festival founder Crayton with Fickling Sr. during 1984 festival. (Photo by Beau Cabell)

Crayton got full participation from her Wesleyan Woods neighbors to plant cherry trees on a cold Saturday morning in November 1973. (Courtesy of Cherry Blossom Festival)

They used plans from a house they had admired in Greensboro. William A. Fickling, Sr., had developed Wesleyan Woods, and he had three cherry trees sent as a housewarming gift.

When the Craytons moved into their new house in July, it truly was a housewarming. It was 102 degrees. Welcome to Macon.

There was actually a welcome sign on the marquee at the Howard Johnson's Motel on Riverside Drive, where Lee stayed while the house was constructed. When the moving van made it to the house, neighbors started dropping by to greet the family. Somebody brought watermelon. The minister of music at a local church came by to invite them to services.

As Carolyn got settled in her new community, she began working for Rivers, who was building houses. She designed the interiors and selected the brick, roof, and floor.

Carolyn embraced Macon. She put down roots. When people introduced her as the "lady from up North," she laughed.

"Yeah," she would tell them. "North Carolina."

She worked at learning to speak the local language, to emulate that distinctive Macon drawl.

She also got involved with the Macon-Bibb County Beautification Commission, the Federated Garden Club, and the Vineville Garden Club. In February 1972, with a major sponsorship from C&S Bank, a "Mother's Mile of Roses" was planted along the fence running from Wimbish Road to Pierce Avenue. They were placed there both in memory of and in honor of mothers. About 3,000 roses were eventually planted along stretches of the interstate north of downtown.

Carolyn's life—and the life of the community—changed forever when she attended a company picnic at the Fickling farm on Rivoli in 1973. Their daughter, Annette, had been working at Fickling's office after school in the afternoons. She asked her parents to attend with her.

At the picnic, Fickling walked over and sat down.

"When we first came here, my husband took us by your house when the cherry trees were blooming, and I fell in love with Macon after seeing those beautiful trees," Carolyn told Fickling. "We live on Guerry Drive, and I have dreamed about our streets out in Wesleyan Woods being lined with cherry trees."

"You know what?" Fickling replied. "I can make that dream come true. If you can make arrangements to plant them, I will give you the trees."

Carolyn went back and told all her neighbors. She received 100 percent participation from the sixty-six homeowners. She called the county to make sure of the rules of the right-of-way. She asked Georgia Power to dig holes 8 feet from the road and 30 feet apart. She asked Rivers to donate the topsoil and pile it on every corner. Phillips Garden Center and K-Mart donated the peat moss.

John Clark of the Georgia Forestry Commission provided instructions on how to plant the trees. A note was placed in everybody's mailbox about the mass planting. There would be a party to celebrate.

On a cold Saturday morning in November 1973, some of the men in the neighborhood borrowed a truck and distributed the 500 trees, a gift from Fickling.

"It was so much fun," said Carolyn. "Some of the children had wheelbarrows. Those trees weren't much bigger than switches. We had big holes and soft dirt, and we didn't plant them any deeper than their roots. The TV and media came out. It was thrilling."

Two other visitors dropped by that morning while the trees were being planted. William and Claudia Fickling drove by to see the shovels being turned and dirt tamped down.

"There were tears in their eyes," Carolyn said. "Mr. Fickling said he would make me a promise. He said he would continue to give me trees for as long as he lived."

And he did.

Crayton conducts litter study with Christopher Gilson, a consultant from New York, as part of the Macon-Bibb County Clean Community Commission (Courtesy of **Macon Telegraph**)

TALKING TRASH

Everywhere she looked, Carolyn Crayton saw beauty.

She found it in the Yoshino cherry trees, in cloud nine dogwoods, and in Southern magnolias. She observed it in those red, running roses she was responsible for having planted along I-75. They grew lovelier each year.

As a member of the Federated Garden Club in Macon, she headed up the club's beautification and civic improvement committee. She convinced local banks to contribute 10,000 tulips to plant downtown at parks and businesses.

But all the beauty that sprung from the ground was often marred by the trash scattered around it.

So Crayton took it upon herself to start a crusade against litterbugs. All she needed was a cape, and folks could have called her Superwoman.

She was familiar with Keep America Beautiful, which was founded in 1953 to address the growing problem of highway litter.

Crayton founded Keep Macon-Bibb Beautiful, which would emerge to provide the framework, foundation, and impressive volunteer network necessary for the creation of the Cherry Blossom Festival.

On a rainy Wednesday afternoon in March 1974, Crayton invited Keep America Beautiful officials to meet with local civic leaders. A presentation was given on the third floor of the C&S bank building at the corner of Cherry and Third.

But they did more than talk about the opportunities. They made a surprise announcement.

Macon had been selected, along with Tampa, Florida, and Charlotte, North Carolina, as one of three national test sites to participate in an eighteen-month litter reduction program. It would differ from past efforts that concentrated on cleaning up existing trash and clutter. The pilot program focused on eliminating the sources of litter.

Crayton was named executive director, and a twenty-eight-member board was appointed. Its mission statement was to "promote public interest in the general improvement of the environment of Macon and Bibb County and to coordinate programs for litter control, beautification, recycling and energy related needs."

Carolyn rolled up her sleeves and met the challenge. She scheduled workshops for civic organizations and interested persons in the community. She reached out to the media and public safety employees.

She asked the health department to do litter counts, and a behavioral scientist was brought in for eighteen months to teach local leaders how to implement the program.

"I carried a clipboard around with me at all times, making notes," she said. "We had to keep up our own yards and help others. There was a lot of paper around flower beds and vacant lots where people had thrown bottles and cans."

She went to Fickling's office to ask for support for her efforts. She pointed out the successes of the program and cited several of the eyesores around town. She complained about a lot at the corner of Forsyth and Tucker roads, where some old buildings were being torn down near Wesleyan College.

She had no idea that the property she was fussing about belonged to Fickling.

"He looked at me and said, 'Well, it sounds like I've got a lot of work to do,'" she said.

Fickling did his part by cleaning up the lot. Showing a sense of humor, he placed a sign along Forsyth Road: "Is this OK, Carolyn?"

Carolyn could never have bought that kind of publicity. Not only did the sign bring a chuckle to those who knew how passionate she was; it also raised the curiosity level of others. It helped spread the message.

Soon, bumper stickers began appearing around town that said, "Carolyn Needs Your Help."

Years later, she would tell a funny story on ABC's *Good Morning, America* about how Macon newspaper editor Joe Parham once stopped to get a New York-style hot dog from a vendor on Mulberry Street.

"Oh, my goodness, Carolyn is looking," Parham said. "I think I'll just go ahead and eat the wrapper, too."

The first litter reduction results reported an 11 percent drop. Then it doubled to 22 percent. As local awareness was raised, the changing attitudes eventually were responsible for an 82 percent reduction in litter across the city. More than 1,300 junk-strewn lots were cleaned, and more than 1,600 dilapidated buildings were torn down. The accomplishments merited a full-page story in *Time* magazine.

The magazine noted Keep Macon-Bibb Beautiful's innovative volunteer program of some 3,000 members and lauded its "systematic approach to identifying environmental problems, reaching out to the community for solutions and providing plenty of positive reinforcement" as it was being held up as a model for other cities.

Dee Newton, who chaired the commission's park committee, told *Time* that the community's attitude had done an about-face. "In Macon, we no longer think of throwing a gum wrapper on the street or trampling on plants," she said.

Later, Keep America Beautiful representatives from Charlotte and Tampa came to Macon, where the program's first handbook was written.

By the late 1970s, the pilot program had been implemented in 240 cities in 35 states and 6 foreign countries. In 1982, Macon was presented with the International Clean Cities Award, the first international award presented by Keep America Beautiful.

The commission later formed energy conservation and recycling projects. Businesses "adopted" downtown blocks and took responsibility for keeping them clean.

Keep Macon-Bibb Beautiful is best known as the springboard to assure that springtime in Macon would be a special time.

Macon may be the prettiest place on earth when the cherry blossoms come out in the spring. (Photo by Beau Cabell)

THE CHERRY TREE BRIGADE

Long before there were cherry trees in the Third Street Park, there were crepe myrtles.

They were pretty, but not so breathtaking that people would come from miles around to marvel at their beauty and drip ice cream beneath their branches.

Kathryn Brown always took a measure of pride in the Yoshino cherry trees that eventually lined the park. She had a role in the emergence of the trees as part of Macon's March marquee.

Brown, who died in 2005, was always in awe of the ornamental cherries. She fell in love with them when she was a teenager living in Washington, DC. She could later make the claim to have lived in both cherry blossom capitals.

Her family moved to Washington from Atlanta in the late 1920s. On outings in the spring, her father went to baseball games while she and her mother read books in the park.

"When the cherry blossoms were blooming, it was always so beautiful," Brown said in an interview in 2002.

She carried that memory with her when she married Smith Wilson "Bill" Brown in 1934. He worked at her father's service station and then at the Ford Motor Company in Hapeville.

They relocated to Macon when Bill got a job as a welder at Robins Air Force Base, moving into a four-room house on Dewey Street in South Macon. Brown said she was reluctant to move there. The surroundings didn't help.

A couple picnics on Coleman Hill during 1998 festival. (Photo by Beau Cabell)

"There wasn't a tree or shrub anywhere," she said. "I had always been interested in growing things. My mother never cut off a limb without rooting it in a pot."

So Brown got together with other women in the neighborhood and planned what to plant. She started the Houston Heights Garden Club, which not only brought beauty to the area but also took on other beautification projects around the city.

Brown worked at the Bibb County courthouse for twelve years and met William Fickling, Sr., one day in the records room.

"We talked about when I lived in Washington, DC," she said. "I told him I wanted our garden club to plant cherry trees in the Third Street Park."

Fickling donated the trees, and Brown and other garden club members not only planted them but also took responsibility to make sure they were watered and fertilized.

Those original trees, planted in 1972, are no longer living. But the festival owes a debt of gratitude to the faith of Kathryn Brown.

With a last name like Woods, it somehow seems appropriate that Jimmy Woods resides on the corner of Timberlane and Wesleyan drives, not far from Wesleyan Woods.

He has lived up to his last name, too. After all, he has been responsible for many of the beautiful Yoshino cherry trees that transformed Macon into the cherry blossom capital of the world.

Several cherry trees stand in his yard. Some of the prettiest Yoshinos in the city are in the surrounding neighborhoods.

Some years during the festival, traffic is jammed along the streets off Wesleyan Drive as people stop to admire the blossoms and take photographs.

Woods's fingerprints are all over some of those trees — and thousands more across town.

He has had a hand in many of them since the beginning of the festival. He can't be sure how many, but he estimates that he gave away more than 200 trees every year from 1982 until 2005.

David Sanders climbs cherry tree downtown during 1988 festival. (Courtesy of **Macon Telegraph**)

He helped plant forty-three trees on Timberlane. As a member of the Southside Lions Club, he also coordinated a project to plant 500 cherry trees along a 6-mile stretch of Eisenhower Parkway from Second Street to Macon State College (now Middle Georgia State College).

More than 12,000 trees were planted between November 1982 and February 1983 under the supervision of county engineer Bob Fountain. The trees found homes in parks, recreation complexes, and cemeteries. Tom McMoreland, commissioner of the state department of transportation, also granted a permit to allow the trees to be planted along all I-75 interchanges in the Macon area.

Woods would drive out to Fickling's farm and pick up trees to distribute around town. Not only did he give them to anyone willing to dig a hole; he also encouraged their tree-planting efforts.

He drew the plans for the Eisenhower Parkway tree project on a napkin at McDonald's after meeting with a DOT official.

Woods moved to Macon in 1945 after serving in the army. He owned and operated Acme Sign Service from 1951 to 2006. He both coined a phrase and designed signs bearing the words "Enjoy the Scene, Keep Macon Clean" for the Keep Macon-Bibb Beautiful commission.

(A commercial artist, Woods also designed the huge sign that counted down the days to the movie, *God Is My Co-Pilot*. This life story of Macon native General Robert L. Scott had its world premiere at the Grand Theatre—now the Grand Opera House—in 1945.)

But perhaps Jimmy Woods's most famous "design" makes him the answer to a local trivia question.

He designed the first Cherry Blossom Festival pin in 1983.

For Woods, some of the most special cherry trees are the ones at his church, Mikado Baptist on Houston Road. They were planted in memory of his wife, Mary, who died in 1994.

He cherishes the beauty of Macon's cherry trees during the third week of March.

He feels blessed to have been a part of it.

For many years, it was easy to pick out Rosa Spivey in the carpool lane.

She usually had a bucket of rooted cuttings of Yoshino cherry trees in the back seat. Rosa was among a small army of volunteers who started planting the trees all over town in the late 1970s.

Yoshinos aren't the only trees that have provided shade in Spivey's garden.

"I've got green genes," she said, laughing. "My family and I love to see things growing."

Spivey has probably plugged more holes and run her fingers through more dirt than any other lady inside the Bibb County line.

She has served as chairman of Macon's Tree Committee, making recommendations for planting locations and species selection.

She also founded the city's Memorial Tree Program. Thousands of oaks, cherry trees, dogwoods, magnolias, maples, oaks, pear trees, and crabapples have been planted in someone's memory.

Washington Park is one of the prettiest spots in the downtown area. People have weddings and picnics with flowers and waterfalls as a backdrop. When the park fell into disrepair, Spivey adopted it as her own special project and helped return it to its former glory. A tree was planted there in her honor.

After attending a conference with Carolyn Crayton, it was Spivey who suggested a new moniker for Macon: "A City in a Park."

She also initiated a project at the Museum of Arts and Sciences, helping to create an educational path and garden of native plants and trees called the Sweet Gum Trail.

There are plenty of gardeners on her family tree, too. Spivey said that she has always been "connected to the ground." She credits her mother, Hazel Schofield, with giving her the passion for growing things.

Her family lived in Stanislaus, and her mother was active in the Vineville Garden Club. A photograph of their yard once appeared on the cover of *Southern Living* magazine.

In 2007, Spivey was given the "Scotts Give Back to Grow Award" for lifetime achievement and was recognized at the prestigious Philadelphia Flower Show in Pennsylvania.

William Fickling, Sr., continued to give away trees almost as quickly as people in the community could plant them. He sent clippings from his trees to a nursery in Tennessee that would root them.

He gave 250 trees to the 236 members of the Georgia General Assembly. He presented nine to Governor Joe Frank Harris and the Governor's Mansion on West Paces Ferry in Atlanta. One was planted on the southeast lawn, and the others were planted along the front.

"Joe Frank wouldn't have any lawn to mow if I planted all the trees I wanted," First Lady Elizabeth Harris said, laughing.

By 1982, Fickling had given away an estimated 30,000 trees. They had been planted in yards and parks and around airports, hospitals, and factories.

Crayton had another dream.

"I told him we wanted to have a weekend to thank him," she said. "We had planned thirty events in honor of the 30,000 trees."

The man she often called "Daddy Bill" was humble, so it took some arm-twisting. He finally consented. The three-day celebration was scheduled at the Candler Building on the campus of Wesleyan College the weekend prior to his seventy-ninth birthday on March 23.

The event was so well received Crayton could hardly contain her excitement. She went back to see Fickling and his wife, Claudia, and told them she wanted to make it an annual event, a full-fledged festival.

"It was just going to be that weekend," she said. "But it was so beautiful and so successful, I couldn't turn it loose."

Willard Scott, the affable weatherman from NBC's **The Today Show** gave the festival instant credibility when he attended the first year. (Courtesy of Cherry Blossom Festival)

FIRST FRUITS

There were no guarantees, no magic formulas for success, no insurance policies to guard against failure. There was no instruction manual tucked away in a drawer somewhere.

There wasn't any money, either. "We started without a penny," said Carolyn Crayton.

But this new festival to pay homage to the cherry blossoms sunk its roots into the ground. Everyone realized the challenges of transforming a long weekend into a weeklong celebration.

The unique partnership that united Fickling's generosity with Crayton's vision would prove to be a terrific marriage.

Crayton was encouraged by the good vibes of the three-day tribute to Fickling in 1982.

"Immediately after it was over, I started thinking about an annual festival," she said. "I had so many people come up and tell me we had to continue it. And I told them we would keep working at it."

A festival office was provided rent-free on the fifteenth floor of the Georgia Power Building (now the Fickling Building) in downtown Macon. The furnishings were sparse—a desk, a phone, and a borrowed typewriter.

Crayton may have had the bare necessities to run an office, but at least she had the resources of a Keep Macon-Bibb Beautiful board and a stable of tireless volunteers. So she wasn't exactly on a high wire without a net.

"I don't know if I ever considered it a leap of faith," said Crayton. "I just knew this was an opportunity for all of us in Macon to do something special."

Although there were thousands of pretty trees to show off, the festival was a neophyte on the spring calendar. There was no sense of identity, no track record to build upon or tradition to follow.

The challenge was to schedule enough events to appeal to everybody. They had to get the folks over in Bloomfield excited about the blooms. They had to attract the day-trippers from Roswell and Thomaston and make them want to stay for supper. They had to charm the charters from Ohio and Texas and put heads on pillows in the local hotels.

"We didn't have anything to market in the beginning," Crayton said. "We had to get out and tell the story."

The festival was so young and unproven that it was paired with a trip to Callaway Gardens as a hook to attract tourists.

Janice Marshall began in her position as executive director of the Macon-Bibb County Convention & Visitors Bureau one month before the first festival in 1983. She remembered some tough sells in the beginning. When she introduced herself, a tour operator thought she hailed from the home of *Macon County Line*, a less-than-flattering redneck action movie from the 1970s. It was a negative image that had to be overcome.

Crayton assembled a committee to help her navigate the course. It included Fickling, businessman Emmett Barnes and his wife, Edwina, Mercer University president Kirby Godsey, and Mercer vice president Emily Myers. She assembled a legal team of Frank Jones and Buck Melton. And she asked William Simmons, president of First National Bank (now Suntrust), to serve as chairman of the first festival.

With her supporters' blessings, the festival registered with the International Festivals and Events Association (IFEA), which provides special-event resources to its more than 2,400 members. The affiliation proved invaluable. Crayton attended the annual conference in Knoxville, Tennessee, and came back with a notebook full of ideas and contacts.

Among the suggestions was the value of a festival pin. It was something people could wear with pride. But it also had value as a promotional tool. Even better, it was a way to generate some much-needed revenue.

So it was off to the races. Literally. Crayton tapped into the pin prowess of the Kentucky Derby and the Indianapolis 500, as well as the Tournament of Roses.

"The Kentucky Derby had the best pin program," she said. "We patterned ourselves after the way they did it. They were great mentors."

Another stream of revenue was provided by cherry blossom flags designed and printed by two local Japanese companies, Textprint and TKG. The flag design was blossoms floating across a silky fabric.

"That first year, we didn't even have a brochure," said Crayton. "We needed something for the tourist groups and visitor centers. We had no money to do anything like that. But Emily Myers at Mercer told me to get the information, and they would get it printed."

Crayton used every opportunity to get the word out and gathered momentum as she learned. She shared plans for the festival at Keep Macon-Bibb Beautiful workshops. She had contacts at radio stations and media outlets in Atlanta, Chattanooga, Savannah, and Augusta.

"They would invite me to come on the shows and tell them what we were doing in Macon," she said. "I would invite people to come to the festival."

There were other news-making events that helped the vision to thrive. Mayor George Israel kicked off the first festival with a declaration: "Some 100 years from

President George H.W. Bush visited Macon prior to the 1984 festival and planted a cherry tree in Third Street Park. (Courtesy of **Macon Telegraph**)

today, may we find our descendants carrying the tradition on and on," he said. "We can take pride that we started it here today."

A dedication was held in Third Street Park of an 8-foot Ishidoro decorative lantern. It weighed three tons and was hand carved from solid granite by craftsmen in Macon's sister city of Kurobe, Japan. It took six months to carve.

And Georgia congressman J. Roy Rowland had Macon recognized as the "Cherry Blossom Capital of the US" in the 1983 Congressional Record. It was a bold move considering Washington, DC, was home of the National Cherry Blossom Festival.

After the festival, the *New York Times* reported that Rowland "broke the bad news to the city [of Washington] a few days ago: Washington is no longer the cherry tree capital of the nation. That title, according to Mr. Rowland, now belongs to Macon, Ga., which recently held its own cherry blossom festival around the 30,000 Japanese cherry trees in and around the city. Washington has only 3,000."

A little love in the *New York Times* was certainly nice, but the bellwether of credibility came when Willard Scott, the affable weatherman from NBC's *The Today Show*, accepted an invitation to attend the festival.

That got everybody's attention.

In time, the festival would attract movie stars, celebrities, Olympic athletes, legendary musicians, and US presidents. But Scott provided the personality and initial star power to take things to another level.

Scott, a self-professed wise guy, was as much of a folk hero as he was a meteorologist. NBC would send him into the heartland to plug hometown events. The inaugural Cherry Blossom Festival was made to order, and Crayton issued Scott an invitation by sending him one of Fickling's cherry trees in October 1982.

It almost didn't happen. On the first day of the festival, Scott was supposed to attend a dinner party in his honor at the home of Emmett and Edwina Barnes. But he couldn't get out of New York because the Atlanta airport, of all places, was closed due to snow and ice. Also stuck in New York was Will Manning, president of the Bibb Company, who was supposed to host the ball the next night.

But Bill Fickling, Jr., came to the rescue when he sent a private jet to pick up the two men. Crayton was there to meet them at the Macon airport in a long, gray limousine. It was cold and blustery. She would later claim that when Scott stepped off the plane, "a golden ray of sunshine burst through the clouds."

At dinner, Scott was seated in the lavish dining room. He took a look at the flower arrangement on the table and turned to Crayton.

"Is this the way you dine every night?" he asked.

"No," said Crayton. "But these are special times."

Special times indeed.

It hardly seemed to matter at 7:00 a.m. on a frigid Monday morning when Scott did his live broadcast, and there wasn't a blossom to be found on the trees in Third Street Park. A few snow flurries started coming down.

Crayton wasn't just shaking from the cold. She was a bundle of nerves. It was her first appearance on national television.

It wasn't long before she found herself in New York for a "live" appearance on ABC's *Good Morning, America*.

"When I thought about this small-town girl going to New York to be on national TV, I couldn't sleep a wink the night before," she said. "But I was always very nervous. I was nervous for every speech I ever gave. I was never comfortable, even though I was excited and prepared. Lee would help me. He listened, and we would change things. But I always had the feeling I had to try harder."

She retired in 2001 after presiding over nineteen festivals. She cut ribbons, hosted royalty, rode in parades, and became one of Macon's greatest ambassadors. She wasn't afraid to get a little dirt under her fingernails, either. She flew in a helicopter, rode a Clydesdale horse, and went for a swim in a shark tank—all to promote the festival.

"Wherever we have been she has always started something," said Lee. "I'm never surprised at what she can do."

The First Lady of Pink is still recognized at the grocery store and the post office. Folks come up and tell her they know her from TV interviews and newspaper stories— even when she's not wearing pink.

One night at a local Italian restaurant, a lady stopped by her table.

"Are you Carolyn Crayton?" she asked.

Crayton smiled and nodded.

The woman smiled back. "We just want to thank you."

Because of Crayton, generations of school children have never known a spring in Macon without the Cherry Blossom Festival.

Without her, after all, it would be just another week in March.

An Elvis look-alike was most likely wearing his pink-suede shoes on this float during the 1993 parade. (Courtesy of **Macon Telegraph**)

LIFE IN PINKISTAN

When Teddi Wohlford and her husband, Bill, moved to Macon in August 1992, they bought a house on Cole Street in Macon's in-town historic district.

Wohlford, now a well-known local caterer, noticed a pink bow on a neighbor's front door the following spring. She assumed the family had a new arrival—a baby girl.

"I did the Southern thing and baked a pound cake and took it over there," she said. "Nobody was home, so I left a note of congratulations."

Within a week, there were pink bows on just about every door in the neighborhood.

"They were popping up all over the place," said Wohlford.

What was going on? The maternity wards must be downloading baby girls. There must be a run on pink rompers in the infants' department.

"Oh my gosh, Teddi," another neighbor said. "Those pink bows are to celebrate the Cherry Blossom Festival."

Welcome to Pinkistan, where there is an epidemic of pink eye in late March every year.

Do not adjust your retina. The world has been pinkwashed.

Pink houses. Pink blouses. Pink dogs. Pink taxis. Pink flags. Pink canes. Pink wreaths. Pink tablecloths. Pink mulch. Pink port-a-potties. One year, the Macon Transit Authority wheeled out a pink bus. Another time, First Macon Bank offered its customers pink checks.

It's the official dress code and building code. Pink blossoms are stenciled on shop windows and in parking lots, and a permanent pink line runs down the center of Cherry Street. A T-shirt in the festival gift shop reads, "Pink Isn't Just a Color. It's An Attitude."

Festival founder Carolyn Crayton even has a pink garbage can at her home on Guerry Drive and pink utensils in her kitchen.

The town is on fire with the glow of an eternal pink flame. It's as if the gavel has fallen on a Mary Kay convention.

When ABC's *Good Morning America* made one of its many visits to Macon during the 1997 festival, reporter Mindy Moore was fascinated with both the pink poodle and with Crayton, who was decked out in pink from head to toe.

Moore turned to the camera and reported to hosts Charles Gibson and Cynthia McFadden, "As you can see, Cynthia and Charles, everything is pink in Macon."

There is a running joke among festival goers that if you stand still long enough, someone will paint you pink.

Pink poodles have star power during the week of the festival. (Courtesy of William Haun, M&R Marketing)

Buttons urge folks to "Think Pink" by participating in a local campaign that targets businesses, churches, schools, and individuals. Blogs and websites have encouraged people to "Link Pink."

When Crayton attended the International Festival and Events Association in Knoxville, Tennessee, during the early years of the festival, she looked around and saw nearly every color of the rainbow.

"The Prune Festival was purple, and the Tournament of Roses was red," she said.

The Cherry Blossom staked claim to pink as an affirmation that every festival needs a signature color.

Connie Thuente worked at the festival office for twenty years as the senior event coordinator and tourism director. Before that, she spent seven years as a festival volunteer.

She remembers when Crayton visited the Shirley Hills Garden Club to talk about the weekend to honor Fickling in 1982.

The Yellow Cab Co. painted four of their taxis pink for the 1992 festival. (Courtesy of Cherry Blossom Festival)

"She said it was going to be a three-day celebration, and everyone was supposed to wear pink," said Thuente. "I was excited when I heard that. Pink is my favorite color."

Thuente considers pink to be the tie that binds during the festival.

"No matter where you go in town, everyone has something pink," she said. "And they do it without being asked. It's thrilling to be part of it."

For the past twenty-five years, Chuck Duggan has figured that if the festival can have a pink poodle, then Fountain Car Wash can have a pink puddle. Duggan is the owner of the popular car wash on Hardeman Avenue. Every March, when the festival rolls around, he mixes his secret formula for suds, and Macon's most famous pink fountain springs to life.

There are glorious days when the fountain spews to pink heights of 13 feet. When the wind is blowing, Duggan cuts the throttle to a flow of about 5 feet.

A pink trash can outside the festival headquarters on Cherry Street.
(Courtesy of Cherry Blossom Festival)

"I have this fear of cars down on the interstate swerving to miss big blobs of foam," he said, laughing.

He is proud that the pink fountain has become a Macon tradition when the Yoshinos are blooming.

"People start calling about two or three weeks before the festival, wanting to know when we're going to turn it pink," he said.

The curious sometimes pull over to take photographs. An entire busload of Japanese tourists once stopped and stayed for almost an hour. A few weeks later, Duggan received a phone call from a Japanese man. "He could barely speak English," he said. "He wanted to know how we made our fountain pink. I told him it was a secret formula. He said he would pay me for it, but I still wouldn't tell him."

That wasn't the only time Duggan has been approached about the chemistry of his pink elixir. He has made a few suggestions but declined to divulge the ingredients. He considers it top secret, like the formula for Coca-Cola.

Duggan's original idea in 1989 was to turn the fountain green for St. Patrick's Day. But March 17 fell during the festival, so it made more sense to have perpetual pink for a week than a green fountain for a day.

Trying to improvise a formula to transform the water into a suitable shade of pink was more difficult than Duggan thought. His first attempt was a "bad decision." Then it went from bad to worse.

"I made a super strong batch, and it turned blood red, like something out of a Stephen King movie," he said. "The red dye stained everything it touched. It was a real mess."

He remembers a co-worker trying to drain the red dye from the 3,000-gallon pool. The overflow trickled all the way down Hardeman across the bridge to Interstate 75.

It took a while to stop the "bleeding."

"I finally got [the formula] right," he said. With the help of a friend in the car wash chemical business, the proper blend was discovered. It also was environmentally safe and non-toxic.

In a town with so much pink, pink puddles are right at home.

If there can be a Fountainbleau, then why not a Fountainpinque?

Every spring, the fountain at Fountain Car Wash on Hardeman Avenue, is turned pink to celebrate the festival. (Courtesy of Fountain Car Wash)

This 1998 promotion featured Vernon Colbert (1991 festival chairman), Florence "Miss Blossom" Wood and Tedi the pink poodle.

(Courtesy of Macon-Bibb County Convention & Visitors Bureau)

GOOD PINK VS. BAD PINK

There is good pink and there is bad pink.

GOOD PINK is when a man is brave enough to wear a pink shirt in public and finds himself comfortably surrounded by other men also wearing pink shirts.

BAD PINK is when a man wears a pink shirt to the truck stop over on Interstate 75, where the preferred color is cowboy denim.

GOOD PINK is when you eat a stack of pink pancakes in Central City Park on a Saturday morning during the third week of March.

BAD PINK is when you get a stack of pink waffles you didn't order at a diner on Pio Nono Avenue in the middle of August.

GOOD PINK is the pink line painted down the center of Cherry Street.

BAD PINK is when your spouse paints a pink line down the center of your living room.

GOOD PINK is when you find yourself face to face with a pink poodle at the arts and crafts festival on Mulberry Street.

BAD PINK is when you find yourself face to face with a pink pit bull down on Seventh Street.

GOOD PINK is when you join the 108 other people standing in line for some cherry ice cream in Third Street Park.

BAD PINK is when they run out of cherry, then switch flavors to salmon.

GOOD PINK is when there are very few red marks on your NCAA Basketball Tournament bracket in the office pool.

BAD PINK is when the team you picked to win the championship in the office pool shows up in the Sweet 16 wearing hot pink uniforms.

GOOD PINK is when your boss tells you to take the rest of the day off and go enjoy the festival.

BAD PINK is when your boss hands you a pink slip and tells you to go enjoy the festival but not to worry about coming back.

PIGMENT OF OUR IMAGINATION

If you live in Macon, or have stepped inside the city limits during the third week of March, you know there are at least three dozen acceptable shades of pink.

They are not pigments of your imagination. There are more acceptable shades of pink than flavors at Baskin-Robbins.

There are plenty of pink uniforms, but not a uniform pink. It's enough to keep you awake at night.

The color wheel includes soft pink, hot pink, dusty pink, bubble gum pink, blush pink, Arnold Ziffle pink, baby girl pink, Mary Kay pink, cotton candy pink, Elvis 1955 Cadillac pink, and attic-insulation pink. Even fuchsia is a permissible pink.

It's like playing a game of "Guess Hue." Only the colorblind are spared.

Pink was a prominent Macon complexion long before there was a Cherry Blossom Festival. It dates back to the founding of the world's first sororities, Alpha Delta Pi and Phi Mu, at Wesleyan, the first college in the world to grant degrees to women. The official color for Phi Mu is pink, of course.

So what is the "official" pink of the festival? Is it two cups of Yoshinos with a dash of vanilla and a big cherry on top?

If you ask Wade Williams, he will tell you it is Tutti Frutti.

Williams is the manager at Acme Paint and Decorating, the headquarters of the "Think Pink" campaign and the festival's "official" paint store.

In the Glidden Paint section, you can pull samples of every pink from Valentine Pink to Tickled Pink to Patina Pink, along with Puppy Love, Cactus Dahlia, Rose Velvet, and Peppermint Candy.

Tutti Frutti has nothing to do with the song by Macon's own Little Richard, a goodwill ambassador for the Macon-Bibb County Convention & Visitor's Bureau.

But it has been the preferred pink for the past several years after festival officials approached Williams with a request for a darker, more full-bodied pink to use at festival venues.

So Williams now takes a tint called Fast Red, adds Magenta and Titanium Red to the mix, and gives it a good shake.

A whole lotta shakin' goin' on.

He doesn't even need a primer.

It's the official color you will find on all festival venues. If you look down at your feet, it's the same shade the city uses to line the streets and parking lots.

Tutti Frutti may be the preferred flavor on the color chart, but it is not the only satisfactory pink.

There won't be any demerits for vagabond shades of amaranth and pixie dust.

Peggy Whyte paints blossoms on windows of businesses and cars weeks before festival. (Courtesy of Roy Shults)

GUY'S GUIDE TO PINK

Pink blouses. Pink skirts. Pink purses. Pink earrings to complement those pink scarves.

Pink pumps to accent pink toenails. Pink pillbox hats for classy heads. Pink umbrellas and pink raincoats to endure those wet days at the park.

Even a fashion show every year to flaunt all that pink.

Festival founder Carolyn Crayton has one of the most extensive pink wardrobes in the fashion world. There is enough to fill three closets with more than 200 pink outfits, coats, hats, purses, shoes, and boots.

It's more of an adjustment for the guys. They have had to warm up to the idea of wearing a polo the color of a medium-rare steak and keep looking over their shoulders for the fashion police.

They don't have to swallow hard to digest pink pancakes in the park or drink from a plastic pink cup.

But it takes guts to wear a pink button-down shirt, pink suspenders, and pink ties with enough flowers to attract a few bees.

Pink has never been the primary color in most men's wardrobes. So this pink fabric revolution has not been a simple evolution for the male population of Macon.

Call it a macho thing. Football teams don't wear pink jerseys. There are no pink stripes on a Marine's uniform. No man has aspired to become a pink-belt in karate.

Macon Mayor Robert Reichert, right, and Charles Jay, second from right, are among the brave men who wear pink during the festival. (Photo by Beau Cabell)

And every March, the men of Middle Georgia are issued a pink permission slip. But the Macon Police Department wears cherry blossom patches on its uniforms.

When the blossoms pop out on the trees, the pink ties come out of the closet. It is acceptable to wear a sports coat the color of Pepto-Bismol.

For ten days every spring, pink is vogue, not rogue. Cherry blossom ties, some from well-known designer Carleton Varney, are among the most popular items in the festival gift shop. There is even a T-shirt that says, "Real Men Wear Pink." Georgia Senator Saxby Chambliss was once seen on C-Span wearing a pink blazer.

Thirty years ago, you couldn't find a single guy in Wimbish Woods or Shirley Hills with a drop of pink on their sleeves for fear of being questioned about their manhood.

Wearing pink is not a gray area. Men's natural aversion to the color comes from having been conditioned to keep their distance. But history contends that it hasn't always been this way.

Pink was once considered the preferred color for males, while blue was reserved for females. As a result of the powerful prejudices of Nazi Germany during World War II, the accepted gender colors were reversed.

When Barbie dolls were introduced in 1959 in their pink garb, it became the new norm. Now parents paint their baby boys' nurseries blue and brush on cans of pink for little girls.

Since the inaugural Cherry Blossom Festival, Macon men have carried a disclaimer, thanks to a band of pink pioneers.

Charles Jay was among the trailblazers in pink blazers. He was chairman of the Keep Macon-Bibb Beautiful Commission, the mother ship of the festival in the early years.

Jay owned one of the original powder-pink sports coats in Macon. They were a special order from Brooks Brothers in Palm Beach because there were no pink blazers to be found in Macon or anywhere else in the state.

Jay remembers attending the festival's first news conference at the chamber of commerce when it was announced that the official color of the festival would be pink.

"You've got to be kidding, Charlie," a friend told Jay. "You don't really think we're going to wear that?"

Jay wasn't so sure himself, but he was a team player. He formed a pact with William Fickling, Sr., Bill Simmons, and Lee Crayton. There was strength in numbers.

"We made a vow that we would always wear them at the same time and stick together," Jay said. "We didn't want to go out on our own in them."

They had to have thick skin beneath those pink threads during the early years of the festival. It was difficult enough to face themselves in the mirror. But, when they went out in public, they tried to avoid the stares. They heard the curious whispers and endured the wisecracks.

One year, they traveled to Washington, DC, to a reception for political representatives from Georgia. The pink-clad delegation was in the hotel elevator one night when the door opened and three burly guys hopped on.

It took quick thinking from Jay, an avid Georgia Tech fan, to put some diffusion on any confusion.

"We told them we were members of the University of Georgia wrestling team," Jay said, laughing.

For many years, Don Mims and his wife, Toots, served as chaperones for the Cherry Blossom royal court during the festival. After arriving at an event at the Macon Coliseum one evening, Don politely asked an usher if he could reenter the Coliseum through a certain door.

The man took one look at Mims and said, "Mister, anybody that's wearing a pink coat like that can go anywhere he pleases."

A lone blossom at Macon's Gateway Park in 2001. (Photo by Beau Cabell)

THE TEN COMMANDMENTS OF PINK

I

Thou Shalt Wear Pink.

It is the official dress code. You will find it in solids, stripes, plaids, and polka-dot patterns. You will see splashes of pink on hats, eyeglasses, sweatshirts, sports coats, and socks. Pink is permissible fashion for Macon men the third week of March.

II

Thou Shalt Coax Thy Tardy Blossoms.

Give your local cherry trees a pep talk. Offer them a vitamin. Of course, we can't rush Mother Nature. The lady has her own agenda. But it's much more fun when the blossoms aren't playing possum.

III

Thou Shalt Eat, Drink, and Be Cherry.

It's a giant buffet stretching from the downtown parks to the local restaurants and street-corner vendors. Pink pancakes and cherry ice cream are among the essential nutrients for the week. We promise not to count calories until after the festival.

IV

Thou Shalt Have No Other Dogs Before Thee.

The festival's official mascot is Petals the Poodle. And its celebrity canine are Lacie and Blossom, who might be the most photogenic pink poodles on the planet. If you attend the Mulberry Street Arts and Crafts Festival, you will see a lot of dogs walking people.

V

Thou Shalt Not Pass on a Pink Line.

The famous pink stripe runs down the middle of Cherry Street. But you can draw an imaginary one all over town. In other words, slow down and enjoy the view.

VI

Thou Shalt Be Kind to Visitors.

They spend a lot of money in Macon, and, heaven knows, the local economy could use some infusion. So when you see someone who looks like they might be from Topeka, Kansas, or the Jersey Shore, smother them with so much Southern hospitality that they will go home wondering where we hide all the mean people.

VII

Thou Shalt Be a Tourist in Your Hometown.

Even though you think you've seen it all, you probably haven't. Learn something new. Go somewhere different. Get out the fresh eyes. Explore and enjoy.

VIII

Thou Shalt Not Rain on Our Parade.

With so many outdoor events, we are always grateful for a ten-day stretch of warm, dry weather. We'll take 75 degrees and sunny all the time.

IX

Remember the Sabbath and Keep It Holy.

It has been noted that Macon has more churches per capita than any city in the United States. Many churches open their doors for worship services, tours, or concerts during the festival.

Thou Shalt Not Overlook Macon's Other Beauty.

It's easy to focus on the more than 300,000 flowering cherry trees. But also take time to appreciate the azaleas, dogwoods, tulips, magnolias, wisteria, daffodils, and redbuds. Few places can leave you as sufficiently breathless as Macon in the springtime.

The pink pancake tradition was started in 1990 by local firefighters as a fund-raiser for the American Cancer Society. (Photo by Beau Cabell)

PINK DOES NOT MEAN MEDIUM RARE

The Cherry Blossom Festival begins every year when the ribbon is cut at the opening ceremonies.

But there are folks—especially hungry ones—who would argue that the festival doesn't officially begin until the first pancake is flipped at Central City Park on Saturday morning.

These aren't just any pancakes. They are made in shades of bubble gum and tutti frutti.

Long before the sun comes up along the levee, dozens of Macon-Bibb County firefighters are stirring the batter and firing up the propane. With several thousand flips of the wrist, Middle Georgia becomes Griddle Georgia.

Welcome to the IFOP . . . the International Firehouse of Pancakes.

By the time the first sip of coffee is swallowed and the maple syrup begins to flow, a line will start forming around the Round Building at the park. You can hear stomachs growling all the way down at the gazebo.

Pink pancakes.

Pink on the outside. Pink on the inside. But never medium rare.

The pancake tradition was started in 1990 by the late Jimmy Hinson, who was fire chief for twenty-four years. The event has always been a fundraiser, with proceeds going to the American Cancer Society.

Hinson borrowed a secret recipe passed down to the department by former Macon fireman L. A. Williams. While serving in the Navy during

Artist Mike Morgan had fun with petals on the grill in 1985. (Courtesy of **Macon Telegraph**)

World War II, Williams was asked to whip up some pancakes for President Franklin D. Roosevelt during one of his visits to the Little White House in Warm Springs. FDR enjoyed them so much that he began requesting them.

The half-century-old recipe was an instant hit in Macon, too. After flipping almost 1,000 pancakes with a pinkish hue that first year, Hinson looked down the long serving line and laughed. "I think we've created a monster."

The monster has grown by leaps and second helpings. The firefighters prepare breakfast for thousands of festival-goers on both Saturday mornings of the festival. The pancake operation is tried and true. It has become so specialized that there are mixers, squirters, cooks, flippers, and servers.

They arrive at the park as early as 3:30 a.m. to start mixing the batter. The pancakes are prepared on revolving, custom-made cookers with electric motors, transmissions, and fly wheels. About fifteen pancakes can be cooked at a time on a carousel heated by propane gas at about 300 to 350 degrees.

Each pancake takes about two and a half minutes before it's ready for a fork. (They will serve no pancake before its time.) On average, the firefighters feed about 4,500 people over the two Saturdays. The pancake pantry includes 3,500 gallons of batter, 2,000 pounds of sausage, and 600 gallons of coffee, juice, and milk.

Carolyn Crayton once took several firefighters with her to WXIA-TV in Atlanta to cook pink pancakes "live" on the air during the morning show. She also carried along some pink grits from Krystal restaurant.

"Some people who had seen the show started pulling in the parking lot wanting us to serve them some," she said, laughing.

When ABC's Barbara Walters inquired about the festival on national TV in 1999, she wondered out loud about the unique pancakes.

"What's in them?" she asked. "What makes them pink? It's not cherry blossoms."

Hinson used to laugh and claim that the pancake recipe included "a little red food coloring and a few cherry blossom petals."

He was kidding about the petals, of course. But anyone who has ever lined up for the free cherry ice cream under the trees in Third Street Park has probably had a few petals provide natural toppings when the blossoms start floating in the air.

They don't add much flavor or nutritional value, but they do contribute to the enjoyment.

Laverne Cantrell knows all about the ice cream experience. She dished it out in the park every March from the beginning of the festival in 1983 until she "hung up her scoops" in 2012.

People do love their ice cream cones, especially when the word "free" is in front of them. They line up in both directions, turning Third Street Park into Macon's own Cone-y Island, where taste buds and Yoshino buds live in harmony.

Cantrell spent every festival as one of those lovely "pink ladies," a matriarch of the butterfat brigade who dressed in a pinafore and gave away thousands of ice cream cones over the ten days.

It was a natural fit for her. In 1962, she went to work at Borden Dairy on Pio Nono as secretary for plant manager Claude Winn. She retired in 1995 after thirty-three years with the company.

Crayton approached Winn about supplying ice cream for the festival. At the time, they no longer made ice cream at Borden's in Macon.

Laverne Cantrell, left, dished out ice cream during the festival for 30 years. Shown here with friend, Kay Truitt. (Courtesy of Laverne Cantrell)

So it was made special for the festival at another Borden plant in High Point, North Carolina. The official ice cream of the festival was known as cherry almond supreme. Borden's mascot—Elsie the Cow—made several appearances at the festival over the years.

When Crayton made her pitch to Borden Dairy and Coca-Cola about sponsoring free ice cream and soft drinks in the park, she used the approach of making the festival inclusive.

"I wanted people who couldn't afford to buy a ticket to the ball or the fashion show to feel some ownership in the festival and to know they were a part of it," she said.

After Borden sold its Macon operation in the early 1990s, a succession of other companies stepped up to the plate to keep the tradition going—from Dairyland to Pet Dairies to Kinnett to Mayfield to Bruster's.

Left, **The Telegraph** published **Cherries Galore**, a cookbook, in 1984. (Courtesy of **Macon Telegraph**)
Right, Iris Crews won the "Cooking Pink in the Park" contest for the second straight year. (Photo by Beau Cabell)

Dairyland asked a Nebraska company, Hiland-Roberts, to concoct a secret recipe and ship 800 gallons to the festival. Kinnett put its own spin on the ice cream, with cherry bits and chocolate chip slivers.

Cantrell volunteered every year. She got paid in good will.

Sometimes people would ask her for chocolate, and she would just smile and tell them, "This *is* the Cherry Blossom Festival."

Pancakes and ice cream have never been the only pink appetizers on the menu. Over the years, the festival has inspired imagination in the kitchen.

A "Cherries Galore" cookbook was published by The Macon Telegraph and News for the 1984 festival. It included 232 pages, with more than 400 recipes contributed by readers.

There has been an array of pink cornbread, pink grits, pink doughnuts, and pink banana pudding. And, of course, pink lemonade and even pink orange juice. There have been offerings of cherry muffins, cherry coffee cake, cherry pudding, and cherry cobbler.

Until recent years, Krystal would stir up some pink grits as part of its breakfast fare.

In 1989, Edwards Baking Company hosted a cherry pie-eating contest at Central City Park and issued a press release, just for fun: "George Washington would have to chop down 9.2 million cherry trees to equal the number of cherry pies Americans eat per year. Of course, Yoshinos are non fruit-bearing."

In 2002, the festival gave folks a chance to take a bite out of what was billed as the "World's Largest Cherry Pie."

The pie was 11 feet long and 5 feet wide and took six hours to cook. It was so large that rakes were used to stir and sift the flour. There was enough to feed 2,000 people.

The Julia Brainchild of the pie was Belinda Johnson, the festival's coordinator of events for Central City Park. She borrowed the idea from the annual Peach Festival in Byron and Fort Valley, which boasted the world's largest peach cobbler.

For several years, a "Cooking Pink in the Park" was held, which inspired such creative dishes as pink soup and "chicken cordon pink."

In the giant pink melting pot, there's always plenty of food for thought.

S&S Cafeteria in Macon served cherry pies during the 1998 festival. (Photo by Beau Cabell)

Florence Wood was an icon of the festival dressed as "Miss Blossom." (Photo by Beau Cabell)

MISS BLOSSOM

Florence Wood stood beneath the canopy of cherry trees at Third Street Park on a spring afternoon in 2001. There was a line for free ice cream between the rows of Yoshinos in the park.

There must have been a thousand blossoms in the median between Cherry and Mulberry streets.

Well, one thousand and one if you counted Florence.

She stuck out like a green thumb.

She was wearing her pink-and-green flower costume. Children ran up and hugged her. Tourists posed for photographs with her.

A smile never left her face.

"I don't do this for myself," she said. "I do it for other people. I'm just an old lady with petals."

For twelve years, she was an icon of the Cherry Blossom Festival every March and its unofficial mascot.

She called herself "Miss Blossom."

She was featured on postcards and interviewed by dozens of television crews, magazines, and newspapers from as far away as England.

Wood was just a shy country girl from up the road in Jones County. So being on such a large stage wasn't something she could have ever imagined for herself.

She raised four children as a single mother and worked for twenty-four years as a nurse at Middle Georgia Hospital. She once cared for William A. Fickling, Sr., the man responsible for all the beautiful cherry trees.

After she retired, she moved to McAfee Towers, a senior high-rise apartment on a hill overlooking the city. She made friends with many of the residents there, and the shy girl disappeared whenever she became the life of the party.

She first made a clown outfit to entertain the residents. They enjoyed it so much that she later dressed up as Santa Claus and the Easter Bunny. She went all out the time she took on the role of Dolly Parton, donning a blond wig, pancake makeup, and a short skirt.

But her shining moment came when she first put on that green skirt, white blouse, and five-petal headpiece.

A star was born. She became a regular in the festival parade every year and a fixture at Third Street Park. She did not drive or own a car, so she had to rely on others for transportation or take the city bus.

At least she had plenty of frequent flower miles.

When she "retired" as Miss Blossom in 2006, her costume was almost down to its last threads. It had been loved to death by all those hugs pressing against the petals.

She had to move to Decatur for health reasons, and she begged her doctor to let her go to Macon for the festival the next year. She had a new costume made for the occasion.

Almost as soon as she arrived at the big tent at Central City Park, people began coming up and welcoming her back.

She was so moved that she started crying.

"This is part of my life," she said.

It turned out to be Florence Wood's final festival. She died in 2012 at the age of eighty-five.

Heaven's garden got another flower.

DOG DAYS

Delise Knight was a dog groomer and the owner of Bardel Pet Grooming in Milledgeville. The "Bar" in Bardel was taken from the first three letters of her mother's first name, Barbara Chapman. The "Del" was the first three letters of her own name.

In 1989, Delise and Barbara took a $90 investment and began making dog bows. Bardel Bows, now headquartered in Fort Valley, is the largest supplier of dog bows in the United States.

Barbara often went by another name. For many years, she was "Medi Tedi." She climbed into a bear costume and entertained patients at the Children's Hospital of the Medical Center of Central Georgia. She brought cheer to patients on the cancer ward and was a popular figure with hospital employees.

When Barbara died in 1993, a friend called a grieving Delise and told her she was going to give her a dog. A dog would make a great companion.

But not just any dog. Delise received a white standard male poodle from championship bloodlines. His high pedigree was his father, Whisperwind on a Carousel, the top-winning standard poodle in history.

Delise named him Tedi in honor of her mother's unforgettable bear character that had brought joy to so many people.

From the beginning, it was obvious that Tedi was something special. Delise would walk him near her home in North Macon. In the spring, when the cherry trees were blooming in Wesleyan Woods, Delise would watch cars, vans, and tour buses take slow drives through the neighborhoods to admire the trees.

"I thought it would be cool to have a pink dog," she said. "That would really be eye-catching."

She had been asked many times to dye the white coats of poodles at her grooming business. People wanted all colors and patterns, from layers of three colors on the ears to "USA" etched into the side. She had also been a judge for creative grooming competitions, so there wasn't much she hadn't seen.

In spring 1994, Delise dusted one-year-old Tedi with a nontoxic pastel chalk and informally introduced the first pink poodle to the festival. She made it a point to walk in the neighborhoods around Guerry and Oxford.

"He loved the attention," she said. "He always knew when he was pink."

By the next festival, Delise had wiped the pink chalk off the drawing board and reached for a bottle of Jazzing by Clairol. The color? Fuschia Plum.

"He was very good about his masculinity, although he probably would have preferred for it to be a blueberry festival," Delise said, laughing.

She would shave his back and paint a blossom with water-soluble markers. By the third year, Tedi was a dye-hard pink poodle with a dynamic personality.

Children hugged him. Senior citizens rubbed his head. College students stopped in their tracks to have their photograph taken at his side. (If Facebook and Twitter had been around back in those days, the hashtag "#pinkpoodle" would have been trending.)

There were times when Tedi was surrounded by so many folks that Delise lost sight of him and her husband, Paul.

"It was like having a movie star on a leash," Paul said.

Tedi wasn't a camera hog. But he was clearly a camera dog. He knew how to pose and where to look. "He was super intelligent," said Delise. "He was only limited by what we could teach him."

He was never an "official" part of the festival, although Cherry Blossom officials were thrilled with his presence. They encouraged the Knights to bring him to as many events as they could. Delise and Paul began taking a two-week vacation every March so they could have Tedi participate in large events such as the children's parade and the fashion show.

Tedi, the pink poodle, was "like having a movie star on a leash" said owners Paul and Delise Knight.
(Courtesy of Knight family)

Tedi got airtime on CNN and the Disney Channel. After an appearance on ABC's *Good Morning America*, Delise and Paul took him to Central City Park for an activity that night.

"Someone came up and told us they had seen Tedi on *Good Morning America* that morning and had driven up from Savannah," Delise said. "They said Macon had to be a cool town if it had a pink poodle. And I told them it was a cool town."

The pink hair dye took several months to wash out. Every time the Knights gave Tedi a bath, he lost a little more of his glow. Sometimes, he still had traces of pink around his ears by the time the next festival rolled around.

One year, several months before the start of the festival, Delise was asked if she could dye Tedi early. He was going to be photographed for a promotional advertisement for the Macon-Bibb County Convention Visitors Bureau, along with "Miss Blossom" Florence Wood and former city councilman Vernon Colbert.

"He was depressed for weeks after that because he knew he was pink, and he thought he should be getting up every morning and going somewhere," Delise said. "So we would put him in the car and ride him around. He thought he was supposed to be doing something."

Tedi lived to be 15 years old, which is 105 in dog years, of course. By his final years of the festival, Delise and Paul had moved north of Fort Valley to Pineola Farms.

Macon pet groomers Paul and Alice Williams soon introduced their pink poodle, Casper, to the festival, and the torch was later passed to Lacie and Blossom.

Tedi left a dog legacy. In 2007, the festival announced Petals the Poodle, a new mascot in a dog costume. And Betty Ragland, a longtime festival supporter, came up with her idea of wooden cutouts of pink poodles to be displayed in yards and on porches in 2002.

"Who would have thought something that started on a whim would have turned out like this?" Delise asked. "We are so honored."

Paul and Alice Williams married in 1968 and bought their first poodle a year later. They named her Tammy, after country singer Tammy Wynette. They got another poodle they named Skeeter, after Skeeter Davis, also a country music artist. Their third dog, Dandy, was a rescue dog and was already named.

"When Tammy passed away, I didn't want another poodle," said Paul. "We had her for seventeen years. She was our heart. We don't have children, so our dogs are our children."

But a friend convinced him that if he had never owned a standard poodle, he had never really owned a poodle. So Paul started researching and found a breeder in Texas.

The dog was black. They named him "Spider Man" because he was shipped in a wooden crate, and "when he came out he was all legs."

But the dog that started them on their amazing journey was named Casper. Yes, he was as white as a ghost.

They drove fourteen hours to Pittsburgh, Pennsylvania, to pick him up. They made the breeder promise not to sell him before they got there. On the way home, they snuck him into a motel that didn't allow pets. It was his first big adventure.

Blossom and Lacie give the festival a double dip of pink poodles.
(Courtesy of Williams family)

Casper's father was a champion and his mother was of show quality. Since he was white, and they ran a dog-grooming salon on Pio Nono Avenue, the couple decided to experiment with dying him different colors. He was red, white, and blue for the Fourth of July. He was orange and black for Halloween. They got so carried away with the holidays that it was difficult to keep up with the seasons.

"He ended up being tie-dyed," Paul said, laughing.

Williams knew there was a pink poodle, Tedi, running around at the Cherry Blossom Festival every year. They didn't want to have dueling dogs. Casper's first year turned out to be Tedi's final year wearing a coat of pink.

Alice was an award-winning groomer, and Paul owned a financial company, Tradebank. He was looking to promote his business. They began to think pink.

They first experimented with a coating of cherry Kool-Aid mix. Then they switched to professional food coloring.

"It was the biggest mess," said Paul. "My palms would sometimes stay pink for weeks. We had to cover everything in the house."

But the results were unbelievable.

"When they're white, people will come up and say they're pretty," said Paul. "When they're pink, it's like a magnet. Never in our wildest dreams did we think it would be like this. We thought it would be just a dang dog."

Casper became a mainstay at the festival. Once, a man from Texas walked up to Paul and said, "I drove all the way from Texas to see that darn dog."

In 2002, Paul and Alice got another white, standard poodle from a breeder north of Atlanta. They named her Lacie because of her fur and because she was so prissy. It was the changing of the guard from a male dog to a female.

"We never thought any dog could be as good as Casper, but Lacie has been," he said. "She has never embarrassed us. Boys will be boys. They will hike their legs when you least expect it. And they are also territorial."

Lacie has taken the pink poodle royalty to a new level. She has even had her own car. Paul bought her a 1975 pink Cadillac Eldorado to ride around town. He couldn't afford a convertible, so he had a friend saw off the top and turn it into a roadster.

It was Lacie's car, Paul said, and she knew it. They would take her to the Sonic Drive-In and order French fries, her favorite.

In 2010, Paul brought in an understudy, seventeen-week-old Blossom, to start grooming her as Lacie's heir. But Lacie, who had started slowing down, picked up the pace when she realized some younger legs were coming along.

She's not ready to be put out to pasture yet. "She's the alpha dog," said Paul.

Lacie and Blossom get prepped for the festival wearing a vegetable-based, semi-permanent dye called "Manic Panic." It's the same kind of hair coloring used by punk rockers. It's a three-day process that can take up to eighteen hours to complete.

"We do this as a way of community involvement," said Paul. "It's our way to give back. We were both born here and raised here. I was gone for four years with the Marines, and I promised God if he would get me back he could bury me here."

They have had their photographs taken with Lacie and Blossom thousands of times.

But you wouldn't always know it.

"I've got very few pictures of me or Alice," he said. "I'm always shown from the knee down. Everybody talks to the dog. Nobody talks to me."

Petals was introduced as the festival mascot in November 2007. While focusing on adding new family-friendly activities, officials began looking for a recognizable cos-tumed character that could be used as a goodwill ambassador at local schools and community events.

A company from San Antonio, Texas, created the design. Petals was selected after studying the reactions and responses of children to other animal characters, such as Curious George and Clifford the Big Red Dog.

Betty Ragland is not only one of Macon's most civic-minded citizens; she is also known as the "Poodle Lady."

No, she is not the owner of Lacie and Blossom, the two most photographed pink poodles on the planet. She does not lead a double life as Petals, the festival's 70 percent cotton mascot.

The Poodle Lady doesn't even own a poodle. She has never owned a poodle.

But she is a devout Georgia Bulldog fan, so when you holler "Go Dogs!" you're speaking her language.

Actually, Ragland does have a house full of poodles, all pink and made out of wood.

If she had her way, Macon may one day become the pink poodle center of the universe. Since 2002, Ragland has been a tireless cheerleader for the wooden cutout dogs that sell for $25,

Betty Ragland was senior queen in 2009
(Courtesy of Ragland family)

with proceeds going to the festival. The Middle Georgia Woodworkers Association makes them, and Acme Paint gives them their appropriate color.

There are now so many of them in front yards and porches that Macon might have to apply for a kennel license.

"I love this festival more than anybody," said Ragland, who served as Senior Cherry Blossom Queen in 2009. "I see how happy these poodles make people when they display them."

She lives on Oxford Road, one of the signature stretches of the Cherry Blossom Trail. Her yard is among the most photogenic in the neighborhood. It is where blossoms and wooden poodles come together with another of her passions—daffodils.

Her "family" of wooden poodles are real showstoppers. Tour buses hit the brakes and let people jump off and walk around in front of her house.

A few years ago, she heard a knock on her door. It was two women from Maryland and one from Pennsylvania.

"They told me they had traveled all over the world, and Macon was one of the most beautiful places they had ever seen," said Ragland. "They thought the poodles were so cute, and they wanted to buy one. Those poodles are contagious. Once you see one, you want one."

Another man, from Florida, told her he was going to take home a pink poodle to put in his yard with all his pink flamingos.

Sometimes folks leave miniature stuffed pink poodles in her mailbox or drop them off at her doorstep.

They are her calling card. After all, she is the Poodle Lady.

Petals enjoys a photo opp with (L-R) Angela Cross, Lala Scales, Virginia Cowsert, and Erith Collinsworth in Third Street Park.
(Courtesy of Collinsworth family)

IMPERSONATING A POODLE

*Revised from author Ed Grisamore's column published
in* The Macon Telegraph, *March 23, 2011*

It was impossible to recognize me behind all that pink fur.

But, yes, it was me.

For two fun-filled hours, I got the inside story of Petals the Poodle.

I had my snapshot taken with children dripping ice cream on the grass at Third Street Park. I greeted a pair of "flesh-and-blood" pink poodles, Blossom and Lacie, who were better behaved than I was. (Especially after I accidentally set off the alarm on that white Mercedes convertible.)

At the food tent at Central City Park, I tried to nibble on one little boy's French fries, then snuck up behind unsuspecting District Attorney Greg Winters, who was eating lunch. (I guess I should be glad he didn't prosecute me for impersonating a poodle.)

Later, I made a full-costumed stop in the sanctuary at St. Joseph Catholic Church, where I surprised a tour group.

Dog bless 'em.

I figured it was time to call it a day when I was mistaken for a bunny rabbit.

You view the world differently when your vision is limited to eye sockets covered with black mesh.

I was surprised at the number of folks who spoke to Petals as if he were a guy. (Guess they didn't notice the dress.)

It is even stranger when everybody calls you by name, and you can't answer back. Volunteers who climb inside Petals, the official mascot for the Cherry Blossom Festival, take an oath of silence.

There are other unwritten rules for being the pink poodle. There is no eating or drinking inside Petals. Whining and text messaging are strictly prohibited. Other than that, you have a long leash.

I owe a special thanks to Kayleigh Irby, a senior at Mercer University and a marketing intern with the Cherry Blossom Festival. Kayleigh chauffeured me everywhere I needed to be, held my hand, and kept me from getting run over by a car while crossing the street. She straightened my pink bows and kept my doublewide paws from tripping over all those curbs.

It was Kayleigh who also saved me from the lions and tigers. The trainer at Central City Park had earlier requested that she keep another volunteer out of sight of the cages, lest the big cats confuse poor Petals for some cotton candy.

It's a cat-eat-dog world, you know.

Was it warm inside all that fabric? Well, let's just say there were times when I considered changing my name from "Petals" to "Sweat-als."

The sign at the bank read 86 degrees, and it was at least 10 degrees warmer on the other side of all that heavy pink cotton. That's why Kayleigh provided me with an ice-pack vest and headband, which saved me from melting like all those cherry ice cream cones.

I'm convinced that I had my photograph taken more than 200 times, at least every minute from late morning to early afternoon. I posed with children in strollers, ladies in sun hats, and businessmen wearing pinpoint oxfords and wingtip shoes. So many folks reached for cell phones to snap pictures that my snout is probably all over Facebook by now.

A tense moment came on Third Street when Kayleigh and Lisa McLendon wanted a photo opportunity of me behind the wheel of a convertible on display from Jackson Automotive.

It was embarrassing enough when I reached for the door handle and the alarm went off. Everybody was looking and pointing at me!

Cameraman Perry Smith at WGXA-TV/Fox 24 came over to investigate, so I'll be lucky if I didn't make the evening news. (Or have my mug on file with Crime Stoppers.)

One fellow in the parking lot at St. Joseph was convinced that there are two Petals.

He claimed he had just seen my twin at the park.

Petals also got a hug from Lula Fowler, of Twiggs County, in the parking lot at St. Joseph Catholic Church.
(Courtesy of Cherry Blossom Festival)

Along the way, I danced a few jigs and skipped down a few sidewalks. Not once did I get blamed for the pollen count. I put a lot of smiles on children's faces. (Unfortunately, I terrified a few of the younger ones.)

One of the most memorable moments was meeting with several special-needs groups that were visiting Central City Park. Many of them were in wheelchairs. A few were mentally challenged.

I'm certain I broke a few records on the hug-o-meter, like when the lady stopped me at the crosswalk on Cherry Street and said she sure could use a hug.

I held out my furry arms for lots of them myself.

It was a day when everybody hugged back.

Artist Sterling Everett's **Spring Matinee** celebrates the beauty from the Woodruff House on Coleman Hill.
(Courtesy of Sterling Everett and Jack Schellenberg)

CREATIVE PINKING

Sterling Everett stood on the steps of the Woodruff House and let his eyes move across the city below him. The beauty that almost took his breath away was the same beauty that had inspired his signature view of Macon gently tumbling down Coleman Hill and Mulberry Street.

With the bristles of his brush and the imagination of his palette, he framed that same image with a vase of daffodils inside the door of the historic mansion, against a backdrop of camellias and cherry blossoms. From the white-clothed table in the Woodruff hallway, the observer is swept out the door, across the green grass, and over the tops of the Yoshinos in all their glory. But the view does not stop there. It is blended into the modern high-rise offices and sloped-roof museums, century-old church steeples and courthouse cupolas.

It was spring 2000, and Everett's agent, Jack Schellenberg, named the rich panorama "Spring Matinee." Everett was the official artist of the Cherry Blossom Festival that year. He also held that distinction in 1987, and his 2013 painting was called, appropriately enough, "Macon's Bountiful Beauty."

Everett has also created two commemorative plates. The first was in 2000, when he painted the small gazebo next to the Woodruff House to complement "Spring Matinee." In 2013, the plate was of the gazebo/grandstand in Central City Park.

Every year, the festival commissions artists, most often with local ties, to create the fine prints, commemorative plates, and pins that will be sold by the thousands. Artists like Everett, Mark Ballard, Steve Penley, Butler Brown, Teresa Smith, Catherine Liles, Bonnie Ramsbottom, and Rose Leavell all have large and loyal followings in Macon and Middle Georgia. Others may be lesser known but still turn heads with their creativity.

Everett grew up near Tennille, the youngest of three sons of a Washington County farmer. His artistic talent showed up early in the pages of his coloring books, where he would "draw outside the lines." He survived tragedy at age six, when he was run over by the wheel of a tractor. It broke one arm in eight places and the other in seven. Months of rehabilitation made him focus on learning to draw again.

He studied art at Young Harris College and finished his degree at Georgia College and State University in Milledgeville, a city rich in history and architecture just like Macon.

When he moved to Macon in 1979, his art career found roots by bringing to life the city's spectacular buildings, landscapes, and monuments.

"Macon has beautiful architecture, and I try to showcase it," he said.

For years, he worked on getting the colors of the cherry blossoms as close to perfect as he could. "It's not something you find in nature very often," he said.

He considers the traditional red-white blend to form pink too stark. So he brings together everything from ultra-marine to Van Dyke brown to yellow ochre to form a grayish beige, then soothes it with a red cadmium.

Macon held its first full festival in spring 1983. Two months later, Steve Penley graduated from First Presbyterian Day School.

At the time, each stood at the threshold of a future filled with possibilities. Of course, neither Penley nor festival organizers could have predicted the fame and fortunes of the next three decades.

Penley left Macon to attend the University of Georgia, then moved to New York City to pursue his dream. While waiting for his big break, he worked as a shoe salesman. He later moved to Atlanta, where he gave new meaning to the term "starving artist." He sometimes had to hunt for loose change under the sofa cushions just to have enough money to buy a sandwich.

Macon native and nationally renowned artist Steve Penley painted **Blossoms and Cotton** in his unique style for the 2007 festival. (Courtesy of Steve Penley)

When his longtime friend and high school buddy, Rob Evans, opened a restaurant, he asked Penley if he could display some of his artwork on the walls. It was his first big sale.

Evans was also responsible for Penley attending his first Cherry Blossom Festival event. Penley went to hear Evans play in a band.

Penley considers it a huge honor that he has been commissioned as the festival artist three times, including both the twenty-five-year anniversary in 2007 and the thirty-year anniversary in 2012.

Not that he needs the recognition. His distinctive artwork has been shown on national television programs and featured in books. It has been displayed in exhibits at famous art galleries and museums.

His 2007 painting was called "Blossoms and Cotton." It offered a view from the foot of Cotton Avenue and the statue of the Confederate soldier. Five years later, he turned the other way with a view from the top of Cotton that he named "A Thousand

Words." It's a turn-of-the-century depiction of the famous avenue. With those two paintings, you can say that Penley has now covered Cotton from head to toe.

After the city's forefathers mapped a grid of square blocks and wide boulevards, Cotton got its name from the angular path the cotton wagons would cut across to reach the boats and barges along the Ocmulgee River.

Penley researched dozens of historical photographs and decided on a bird's-eye tableau down Cotton from behind the left shoulder of City Hall. In the distance is the top of the courthouse, First Presbyterian Church, and the Dempsey Hotel.

"I found this one old photograph, and what really got my attention were the street-cars," Penley said. "It was so cool to see them traveling up and down the hill. It sparked my imagination.

"I also love the old buildings and church steeples. The architecture is amazing, and downtown is spectacular. I think Macon is one of the most under-appreciated cities in the South."

Of course, it wouldn't be a painting of the cherry blossoms without some pink-hued trees. Penley had to exercise a bit of artistic license, since the era he was capturing—the early 1900s—was some fifty years before the first cherry trees appeared on the scene.

His title came from the expression "A picture is worth a thousand words." On warm spring days in Macon, thousands of words are necessary to describe the beauty.

Mark Ballard has been the festival's most prolific artist over the years and one of its most popular personalities. He has designed ten plates and ten pins and been selected for two fine art printings. He is the only artist to have done all three the same year. His creativity has also turned up on festival T-shirts.

Ballard grew up in Macon, and when he moved back home from Atlanta in 1986, he said he was looking for ways to get involved in the art community.

He took photographs of the Fickling home on Ingleside and presented Fickling with a painting on Founder's Day. That was when he met festival director Carolyn Crayton and Fickling's daughter-in-law, Neva Fickling, who was Miss America 1953. He became close friends with both women. Crayton asked him to do the artwork for the festival in 1987.

Local artist Mark Ballard has designed plates and pins for the festival over the years. (Courtesy of Mark Ballard)

"I have never gotten tired of the cherry blossoms," Ballard said. "It's the most wonderful time of the year in Macon. I love the color and the shape of the blossoms. Even the buds are beautiful."

The multi-talented Ballard has also become a mainstay at the festival as emcee of the fashion show, with the help of his wife, Debra. He selects the clothes for the models and also designs everything from the backdrops to the centerpieces on the tables.

Of all the artists who have been commissioned for the festival, Teresa Smith is the only one who can claim to have been a former Miss Alaska.

She made her first appearance on the Wesleyan campus in fall 1962 to study art. It seemed as if the entire student body was there to greet her, curiously waiting for this "foreign" delegate to step out of the car.

"All the girls in my dormitory were out there," she said. "I guess they wanted to see the Eskimo."

Imagine their surprise when Smith, whose maiden name was Teresa Hanson, strolled up the walkway with blond hair flowing down her back.

It's understandable why Smith arrived with considerable fanfare. She was, after all, Miss Alaska 1962 and competed in the Miss USA Pageant. Because Alaska did not become a state until 1959, it took years to thaw the stereotype of igloos and frozen tundra.

"When you live in Alaska all your life, as I did, you are on top of the world, and everything else is 'down there,'" she said. "Whenever somebody from Alaska went to the states [U.S.], they would say they were going 'outside.' Going to Wesleyan gave me a chance to go 'outside.'"

The motto of the state she represented was "North to the Future." Little did Smith realize that her future would be shaped by a trip to the South.

She met and married Bob Lee Smith, a former auto dealership owner and real estate developer. They met when she was asked to crown Miss Macon at the local pageant. He was a local singer who performed as part of the program that night.

She raised a family and became one of the city's renowned artists, painting everything from wildlife to landscapes.

And she painted cherry blossoms.

She has been the official artist of the festival and designed the collector's plates three times.

Peggy Whyte, a local artist and professional sign painter, doesn't paint her blossoms on canvas. They are usually splashed across storefront windows and car windshields.

Her contributions to the festival began in 1992 when Crayton asked her to paint the official car.

She can draw the five-petal blossoms with green leaves as either a single blossom or as multiple blossoms that cover an entire window. Her familiar blossoms usually start appearing weeks before the regular blossoms at the festival's "Think Pink" kick-off at Acme Paint on Riverside Drive in February.

There is more to "creative pinking" than artwork. In 1994, Macon's Murriel Meadows designed a doll in the likeness of festival founder and director Carolyn Crayton. The following year, she added a doll named "Claudia" in honor of Claudia Fickling, the wife of William Fickling, Sr. The doll won first place in the International Festival competition out of more than 2,000 entries.

She next added a doll named "Macon" and, in 1997, a 21-inch fashion doll made of porcelain and named "Georgia."

Festival-goers get a ride in a horse-drawn carriage at Third Street Park in 2001. (Photo by Beau Cabell)

STOP AND SMELL THE CHERRY BLOSSOMS

The tall pine trees stand guard at Rest Area 22, north of the Interstate 75 and 475 split in Monroe County. There is a cluster of cherry trees along the ramp as you leave, a sneak preview of the trail ahead.

The Macon-Bibb County Convention & Visitors Bureau maintains a presence there, where travelers can pick up brochures to the Hay House, Ocmulgee Indian Mounds, and other attractions.

The nearest venue for the Cherry Blossom Festival is a dozen miles away. But make no mistake about it. This is where the Cherry Blossom Trail begins.

This is where you pick up the scent, where you cross the northern perimeter of the pink line. It is the festival's front door, the welcome mat for southbound voyagers.

For the snowbirds who have not seen a blade of green grass in six months, it is an open invitation to the rites of spring.

For the curious, but not committed, it is the persuasion station, the hook that lures them to Macon.

For others, even the hardest sales pitch won't work. The sea breezes of Florida are calling their names. Or they can't wait to get to the Land of the Mouse. Besides, I-475 will put them 5 miles closer to the Promised Land. If they hurry, they can make the early bird dinner special in Ocala.

But those who do stop and smell the cherry blossoms are rewarded.

Macon was lauded as a garden spot long before William Fickling, Sr., discovered those accidental cherry trees growing in his yard in 1949. It is situated along the fall line, a geological boundary that runs from Columbus to Augusta. The line separates the rolling, red-clay hills of the Piedmont region from the flatter terrain and sandy soil of the Coastal Plain.

William Bartram, the famous botanist, passed through in the early 1770s. He took note of the wild hydrangeas and wrote that the "wholesome countryside appeared fertile and could be profitably cultivated."

The Hanging Gardens of Babylon, one of the Seven Wonders of the Ancient World, inspired Macon's early planners. In 1823, James Webb, a local surveyor, began to design a city grid with wide avenues and public parks. In the early years, residents were required by ordinance to plant shade trees in their yards.

Central City Park, now one of the centerpieces of the festival, has been around almost as long as the city of Macon. In 1826, just three years after Macon received its charter, the state legislature designated 273 acres south of Seventh Street for the "purpose of preserving the health of the inhabitants of the city."

Ambrose Baber, one of Macon's founding fathers and a prominent local physician, is credited with initiating the legislation to have the park area designated. One of his main motivations was his belief that the swampy area around the park should be developed because it posed a potential health hazard (as a breeding ground for mosquitoes). He was said to have the "hygienic interest of the town's location in view."

He also wanted to preserve the large trees in the area, and the legislation prevented the trees from being cut and the property from being sold. The park stayed undeveloped for several years and was known as the "city reserve."

Less than a decade later, a trotting park opened and was named the "Central Course." Macon mayor Colonel William A. Huff is credited with much of the vision for the park some fifty years after that. The mayor oversaw the construction of many of the buildings and facilities in preparation for the Georgia State Fair in October 1871, when the area was renamed Central City Park.

In John Campbell Butler's *Historical Record of Macon and Central Georgia*, published in 1879, he described the public park in its early days as " . . . delightfully shaded by a native growth of monster oaks and ornamented with flowers—wild and garden plants—smooth walks and fountains, lakes and river scenery."

a-wop-bop-a-loo-mop-alop-bam
bloom

Macon's own Little Richard does a little tutti frutti to get the trees to bloom.
(Courtesy of Macon-Bibb County Convention & Visitors Bureau)

Third Street Park was also part of the original city planning in the 1820s. The park was used for the tethering and feeding of farmers' horses that brought products to the Macon market. Beautification efforts began in 1913 when a fountain was installed, and iron benches from Central City Park were eventually moved there. The park is actually a series of four smaller parks between the blocks covering about 3 acres. In the early twentieth century, trees, azaleas, and camellias were planted there.

The book *History of Macon: The First One Hundred Years* contains a reference to the American Rose Society, in July 1920, establishing its "official testing and exhibition grounds for the Southeast in Macon. Lands were provided in Baconsfield Park and experts put in charge. This should be an asset to Macon and a valuable addition to the natural beauty of the city."

In February 1922, more than 100 magnolias were planted on Highway 41 in Macon in honor of Bibb County war heroes as part of "Remembrance Road."

The city hosted the first public camellia show in the United States in February 1932 at the Burden, Smith & Co. department store downtown. The Azalea and Camellia Society of America, which later became the American Camellia Society, was organized at the downtown Dempsey Hotel on September 29, 1945. Its forty-eight charter members were mostly made up of members of the Vineville Garden Club.

Macon starts its springtime crescendo in late February and early March and even the florally challenged are impressive. The first tease comes from the Japanese magnolias, sometimes known as the tulip tree. The flowers usually bloom before the heart-shaped leaves spread open.

A tourist takes a photograph at the Sidney Lanier Cottage on High Street. (Courtesy of **Macon Telegraph**)

The daffodils, with their bright yellow colors, also begin to show their faces in February. Another brush of yellow comes from forsythia, sometimes known as golden bells. The butter-colored flowers fill yards like splashes of sunshine. The city of Forsyth, about 15 miles north of Macon, holds a Forsythia Festival in March, one week before the Cherry Blossom Festival.

The redbuds also come out to play early in the partial shade of larger trees. The name is deciduously deceptive, since the clusters of flowers are more purple and pink than red.

The azaleas, dogwoods, and magnolias usually don't make an appearance until after the cherry blossoms have come and gone. There are more than fifteen varieties of azaleas native to the Southeast.

The dogwood, found in all 159 Georgia counties, is an ornamental tree native to the South. Its blossoms are the state flower of Virginia and North Carolina, and its beauty has inspired dogwood festivals in Atlanta and Perry. The Easter legend, prominent in the South, is that the dogwood was the tree used to crucify Jesus on the cross, which is why its petals form the shape of a cross.

The magnolia is one of the most magnificent and aristocratic trees of the region, an evergreen that can grow up to 50 feet tall. Its white blossoms are the state flower of Louisiana and Mississippi.

Other trees that amplify Macon's beauty in the spring are Bradford pear and crabapple trees.

There are a number of Macon residents who have probably never purchased a cherry tree. They have received them through the continued generosity of the Fickling family. Since 1991, the Keep Macon-Bibb Beautiful Commission has also had success with its "Bring One for the Chipper" program in January. Macon families bring their Christmas trees to Central City Park for recycling and receive a free cherry tree seedling in return.

And, since 2006, the city has been replenishing not only the Yoshinos but adding heartier ornamental cherries to the landscape.

Hear him on the cherry tree
From the topmost spray
With a heart brim full of glee
Pouring out of his lay.

From "A Cheerful Singer" by Macon poet Sidney Lanier

A rainy day stroll beneath the Japanese lanterns hanging from the Yoshino trees in Third Street Park in 2003. (Photo by Beau Cabell)

BLOOM WITH A VIEW

On a bus tour during the festival, a woman tugged on the guide's arm and asked how many cherry blossoms her group was going to see.

"Ma'am," he told her, "you're going to see so many Yoshinos you will be counting cherry blossoms in your dreams."

They come from everywhere—from North Dakota to Michigan to Virginia to as far away as Hawaii. They come from small towns and big cities, rural outposts and concrete jungles. Some climb aboard chartered buses making springtime pilgrimages through the South. Others arrive as part of church groups, senior organizations, and school kids on class field trips.

They ride along Macon's tree-named streets—Walnut, Magnolia, Mulberry, and Poplar—to the tree-lined neighborhoods along the festival's Cherry Blossom Trail.

They sip on the city's rich history like a mint julep and marvel at its architecture and commitment to preservation.

But the trees are always the headline act. They come to see the trees.

If you planted the more than 300,000 trees in a single row 10 feet apart, you would have more than 500 miles of beauty from the foot of Cherry Street to the home of the National Cherry Blossom Festival in Washington, DC.

The official festival bus tours leave the shadow of the levee at Central City Park, then make their trek to the Fickling Farm on Rivoli Drive and back. The

A tour bus group visits the Fickling's front yard on the Cherry Blossom Trail. (Photo by Beau Cabell)

trees are the drawing card, the big-ticket item. When they are in full bloom, the tour guides simply let the trees do the talking.

If visitors don't take anything else home—no souvenirs, no history lessons, no overdoses of Southern hospitality—at least they preserve the breathtaking trees in words and photographs.

There are three signature venues along the Cherry Blossom Trail: Third Street Park, the Fickling residence and farm, and the Wesleyan Woods subdivision along Guerry Drive and Oxford Road and Circle.

THIRD STREET PARK. This is the main stage of activities for downtown. There are three blocks of trees along the wide median, stretching from Poplar to Walnut. At their peak, the trees form a tunnel of breathtaking blossoms. So many photographs have been snapped here over the years you might wish you had invested in the picture-post-card business. Many of the daytime ceremonies are held near the stage at Third and Cherry. It is also the place to be at lunchtime, when families bring picnics and spread out on the grass, then wait in line for free cherry ice cream. Fifteen streets, including Cherry Street, are named after trees in downtown Macon. The others are Walnut, Mulberry, Poplar, Plum, Pine, Hemlock, Orange, Magnolia, Hazel, Chestnut, Maple, Elm, Oak, and Ash. For the record, Cherry Street was named long before there was a Cherry Blossom Festival.

THE FICKLING PROPERTIES. Not everyone can claim that their driveway is a tourist stop, but Bill Fickling III can look down the hill at the wide entrance to his driveway and see tour buses parked beside cars with out-of-state license plates. It's not unusual to have visitors wander up the winding driveway and even venture into the yard to get a closer look at the stunning display of trees. This is where it all began, so there is a reverence as if they are walking on holy ground. The property also boasts gorgeous azaleas and dogwoods. The private driveway circles behind the house, where it is known as Melanie Drive, and exits to the back on Ashley Drive. (Ashley and Melanie Wilkes were both characters in Margaret Mitchell's *Gone with the Wind*.) It's a pleasant, ten-minute ride from there to the Fickling Farm at the corner of Rivoli and Northside drives. Visitors can admire the trees, surrounded by a white fence against the backdrop of horses grazing in the pasture.

WESLEYAN WOODS. The dreamiest part of the trail is the 3.8-mile loop along Guerry Drive, Oxford Circle, and Oxford Drive. Guerry is the home of festival founder Carolyn Crayton, who once laughed and said the road could be renamed Cherry Drive. When the blossoms are popping, the beauty there is unrivaled. When they begin to fall to the ground at the end of their bloom cycle, it is like being in a snow globe. No other neighborhood is as invested in the spirit of the festival, with pink bows on mailboxes and pink wreaths on the doors. Betty Ragland, who came up with the idea of the wooden pink poodles, lives on Oxford Circle. On the bookend weekends of the festival, these streets are sometimes filled with sightseers. You might even find young entrepreneurs selling pink lemonade in their driveways. "I don't know what heaven looks like," said a veteran tour guide. "But I like to think it looks a lot like this."

The canopy of trees along Oxford Road provide some of the most breathtaking blossoms on the trail. (Photo by Beau Cabell)

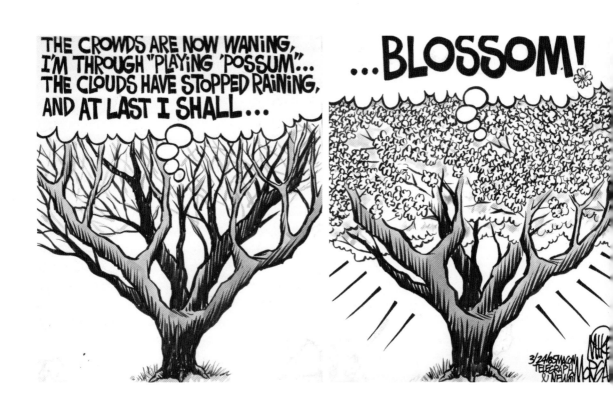

Sometimes the trees play "possum" until the end of the festival. (Artwork by Mike Morgan)

THE BARELY BLOSSOM FESTIVAL

I think that I shall never see
A blossom so welcome on any tree.
We've waited and waited until we're agitated
Because our beloved blooms are much belated.

—*"Ode to a Cherry Tree" by Ed Grisamore*
   (with apologies to Joyce Kilmer)

The weather in March cannot be trusted. It is supposed to roar in like a lion and go out like a lamb.

But it's more like a chameleon. Or a psychotic dog.

Dew on the grass in the morning. Frost on the ground the next day. Flip on the air-conditioner in the afternoon. Turn up the thermostat at night.

One March afternoon you might be bathing in sunshine. By the next morning, you might be taking a different kind of bath. March plays host to Windy Wednesdays and Thunderstorm Thursdays.

Festival organizers have learned they can't control Mother Nature. Everything can be planned to the minute, organized and well-staffed, but the weather has its own agenda.

So do the trees. They can be beautiful show horses. Or they can be as stubborn as mules. Sometimes the Yoshinos are the Yo-shi-no-shows. They tease. They hide. They stall.

Welcome to the Barely Blossom Festival.

Predicting when the trees will bloom has been an inexact science for as long as the festival has been around. The benchmark bloom date is Founders Day on March 23, the birthday of William Fickling, Sr.

But sometimes the buds are more fickle than Fickling.

There have been years when they arrived early. The petals hit the ground before the festival was finished. Other times, they have been fashionably late—tardy to the party. They show up still wearing their pajamas, then hit the snooze button.

A stretch of warm sunshine can nudge them from those winter naps. Likewise, a cold snap can send them into a state of arrested development.

The 1996 festival had it all—sun, rain, cold, wind, snow flurries, and late-blooming trees. There was the usual temptation to push the festival back.

"We are sandwiched between the Bradford pears and the dogwoods," Crayton explained. "If we moved it any farther back, we might have to switch to a dogwood festival."

Bill Fickling III has analyzed the bloom patterns based on his grandfather's journals, coupled with personal observations. His conclusion? The blossoms will make their entrance two weeks on either side of March 23. Actually, the exact median date is March 22, so just call it March 22.5.

The most consistent variation in his studies is "inadequate chill hours."

"Cherries, like peach trees and other stone fruits, require a minimum number of chill hours for a good fruit set," he said. "If they do not receive sufficient chill hours, then the bloom is irregular and delayed."

This still applies, even though the Yoshinos are flowering cherries and bear no fruit. Fickling breaks it down like this:

If the winter is cold followed by a cold spring, there will be a late bloom.

If the winter is cold followed by a warm spring, there will be an early bloom.

If the winter is mild followed by a cold spring, there will be a late bloom.

If the winter is mild followed by a mild spring, there will be an irregular or late bloom.

Fickling has provided festival officials with input on selecting the best dates for the festival, since it always seems to be hit-or-miss. He has advised that it is best to have the beginning of the festival closer to March 23. Also, the dogwoods and azaleas usually bloom after March 23. Their presence can sometimes help ease the pressure if the cherry blossoms are still not cooperating.

When visitors arrive to an empty stage, they often have to use their imagination. One year, a church group from Nashville, Tennessee, traveled to the festival, anxious to see the blossoms. Some members of the group had been to the festival two years earlier, when the trees were peaking, and brought their friends back to see the beauty.

Unfortunately, by the time they got there, the blossoms were making an early exit. Disappointed? Yeah, a little. But they had a wonderful time learning about Macon and its history, so they weren't about to let the vanishing blossoms ruin their visit.

One man said that he had once taken a trip to Alaska but couldn't see Mount McKinley because of all the clouds. But he didn't let it rain on his parade.

Several years ago, Fickling set up a video camera looking out a front window at his house and offered visitors a "bloom cam" on the festival's website.

But most of the time, the festival office handles it the old-fashioned way by answering the hundreds of phone calls with the proverbial question, "Are the trees blooming?"

Connie Howard, the festival's souvenir manager, remembered one year when the Japanese consul called and wanted to know when the trees bloomed. She told him it was usually the third week in March.

"What day?" he asked.

When she told him she had no idea, he asked to speak to the person "in charge of the trees." He said that each tree is registered in Japan, and people are assigned to a tree. They then call a special number to report when their tree is blooming.

Howard laughed. In a city with more than 300,000 Yoshino trees, one can only imagine how that would work out.

Connie Thuente, the festival's former senior event coordinator and tourism director, remembered a receptionist named Monte Blote who could type in time to the radio and always had an answer when the phone rang and someone wanted a blossom forecast.

"She talked straight to everybody," Thuente said. "She told them we don't know. Only God knows for sure."

THIS BUD'S FOR YOU
A TIMELINE OF THE BLOOMS

MARCH 20–27, 1983	Cold and rainy. Blossoms were playing hard to get.
MARCH 18–25, 1984	Blooms were shy at first, then came out to play.
MARCH 17–24, 1985	Late-arriving to the party, and complete no-shows downtown.
MARCH 16–23, 1986	After tardy slips issued again, festival moved to later for the next festival in 1987.
MARCH 20–27, 1987	Even with pushback date, blossoms were slowpokes.
MARCH 20–28, 1988	A few here and a few there but not everywhere.
MARCH 19–25, 1989	Yoshinos decked out by the middle of the week.
MARCH 19–25, 1990	Punctual at the start and spectacular throughout the entire week.
MARCH 15–24, 1991	Didn't come out in all their glory until the end.
MARCH 20–29, 1992	Fashionably late at the start. Pretty in pink at the end.
MARCH 19–28, 1993	Cold snap at start of festival kept them in bed all week.
MARCH 20–27, 1994	On time and in full bloom for the week.
MARCH 17–26, 1995	The blossom possum was at it again.

MARCH 15–24, 1996	A Spring freeze decimated peach crop. Played havoc with cherry blooms.
MARCH 14–23, 1997	Terrific weather and perfect timing. Blossoms everywhere you looked.
MARCH 20–29, 1998	Blossoms put on a show in north sections but delinquent in downtown area.
MARCH 19–28, 1999	Confused by lack of winter cold days, complete shut out for first time.
MARCH 17–26, 2000	On time and beautiful. Fabulous weather after a wet start.
MARCH 16–25, 2001	Trees peaked before festival started. Bummer.
MARCH 15–24, 2002	Weather cooperated but late-arriving blossoms did not.
MARCH 21–30, 2003	Later start helped, but blooms fell before final gavel.
MARCH 19–28, 2004	Festival opened to symphony of blooms. Weather was absolutely splendid.
MARCH 18–27, 2005	Blossoms were average. Had to withstand rough weather.
MARCH 17–26, 2006	Chilly weather at festival beginning and erratic blooms during the week.
MARCH 16–25, 2007	Blossoms were a hit in the end after a shaky start out of the gate.
MARCH 28–APRIL 6, 2008	Latest start ever to festival. Bleak weather put damper on blossoms.
MARCH 20–29, 2009	Blossoms and good weather greeted festival. Stormy finish at end.
MARCH 19–28, 2010	Blossoms were sparse during a frigid opening weekend.
MARCH 18–27, 2011	Nice weather and decent blossoms. Storms ruined finale.
MARCH 16–25, 2012	Rough weather at beginning and end. Blooms tried to hang tough.
MARCH 15–24, 2013	Weather prevented blooms from being at their best.

Members of the Flag City School of Dance carry blossoms during 1999 parade. (Photo courtesy of **Macon Telegraph**)

HOW TO COAX A BLOSSOM

Sweet Talk

It may not help, but it sure won't hurt. Urge the flowers to give it the old—no pun intended—"collage" try. You might need to get a Japanese interpreter. After all, these are Yoshinos. They may not speak the language. Just remember to try this after the sun goes down. You don't want your neighbor saying, "Look, honey. Ralph is out in his yard talking to the trees again!"

Dance

Make sure you push the right button on the jukebox, because rain dances are never popular during festival week. The cherry tango and Yoshino shag are usually effective. When dancing around the tree, though, watch out for low-lying limbs.

Sing

Cherry trees prefer rock 'n' roll, although country, hip-hop, and church hymns are permissible. Festival officials often put their own spin on "Tutti Frutti," a song by Macon's own Little Richard Penniman. A-wop-bop-a-loo-mop-alop-bam-BLOOM!

Be Patient

If all else fails, just remember the greatest virtue of all. Patience. They're like babies. They come when they're ready.

Toot and Don Mims piled up plenty of "frequent flower" miles getting members of the royal court where they needed to go. (Photo by Beau Cabel

HELPING HANDS

The well of volunteerism never seems to run dry.

Connie Thuente said she could not have done her job without the more than 1,000 volunteers who provided the gears for the festival engine. The week before the festival every year, she would look across the City Auditorium with pride at the annual volunteer luncheon.

"It was always full, and everybody was dressed in pink," she said. "They just loved being part of it. It was their way of being involved in the community. We called it 'ownership' of the festival. If they felt that way, they would take care of it."

Sometimes local businesses and banks send teams of volunteers. Other times a local school, church, or college supplies the volunteer pool. For many years, the BellSouth Pioneers placed all the pins in the packets before the festival. For the past few years, Middle Georgia State College (formerly Macon State) has enlisted hundreds of volunteers to help with the balloon glow at the college, one of the festival's most popular events.

"It meant a lot when they would call to say, 'We're going to do this' or 'We're going to take care of that,'" Thuente said. "I would arrange to get the tables, and they would take care of the tablecloths. And I found a lot of my volunteers. God put them in my path."

Super volunteers Charles Jay, Martha Carter, Dee Newton, and Marie Williams were with the festival almost from the beginning.

Jake Ferro, the festival's current director, first got involved as a volunteer. He and his wife, Michele, moved to Macon in 1986, and he served as president of Huber Kaolin. Dr. Aaron Hyatt, the former president of Macon State College, lived across the street and got them involved as co-chairs of the ball.

"There is no way we could put on a festival without a dedicated group of volunteers," Ferro said. "They are the unsung heroes behind the scenes. Some of them schedule their vacations around the festival so they can help. We have a very dedicated board who are all volunteers. We also used interns and others doing in-kind work as volunteers."

At first glance, it was a plain white courtesy van on loan from Riverside Ford. It had four tires, a steering wheel, and a radio. It had air conditioning for warm March afternoons and a heater for cool spring nights.

But, after local artist Peggy Whyte painted cherry blossoms on the windows and "Royalty" on the side, it became a magic bus.

Don and Toots Mims usually had every seat filled with precious cargo—five young ladies dressed in pink from head to toe. They buckled them in and transported them to ribbon cuttings, parades, concerts, and worship services.

In parking lots and at stoplights, folks would often try to sneak a peek through the tinted windows to see the "royalty."

For ten years the couple shuttled the royal entourage to local venues and served as chaperones for the Cherry Blossom queen and princesses. The girls called Toots the "Queen Mother." She had about a dozen pink hats, a different one for every day of the festival.

Without volunteers like them, Macon would have thousands of cherry trees with no festival to celebrate. They perform an important service to this community.

The royal court could search behind every Yoshino in Macon and never find a pair of better role models.

Toots and Don were childhood sweethearts and have been married for more than fifty years. Don retired from S&S Cafeteria. Toots—whose real name is Emily Ann— was a retired teacher who taught at Stratford Academy and Gray Elementary.

Don first got involved with the festival in the early years when S&S was a corporate sponsor at the first Cherry Blossom Ball. Later, after he and Toots both retired, Thuente persuaded them to take on the chaperone duties. Former Macon mayor David Carter and his wife, Martha, had previously served as chaperones.

The Mimses loved every minute of it. Toots said it involved them in parts of the festival they might never have seen otherwise. It introduced them to events they might not have attended.

Their duties were more involved than simply a glorified taxi service. They worked with the young ladies on social graces. Before the festival started, they would invite them to a formal dinner at their home, where etiquette and table manners were taught and rehearsed. It always helps to know which fork to use.

Toots also practiced with them on the art of conversation, learning to look people in the eye and using good diction. She discussed what to wear for different events during the festival. She preached about being wholesome and not wearing jewelry that would detract from their natural beauty.

And the number 1 rule? Never, never, never chew gum.

Don and Toots learned to pace themselves, striving not only to be on time but also early to every event. That helped alleviate a lot of the stress.

They enjoyed meeting people from all over the country and world. They joined others in expanding their horizons. But the true joy was meeting folks who lived and worked right here in Macon.

Alice and Ken Fields attended their first festival in 1983. They went to just one event—a train ride at the Terminal Station.

So they never could have dreamed that, a decade later, they would volunteer for jobs that would make them feel like they were at Grand Central Station during the third week of March.

Or that they would devote boundless energy to making sure thousands of visitors were connected with hundreds of tour buses.

They could be found at the tour booth in the Long Building at Central City Park, where they checked schedules, answered the phone, and arranged for groups to take a three-hour tour of the city—and hopefully see some cherry blossoms along the way.

Ken and Alice Fields pose for photograph with tourist in the Fickling's driveway on Ingleside Avenue.
(Courtesy of Roy Shults)

They were always well stocked with Alice's homemade peanut brittle and legendary sausage biscuits. Many of the tourists would drop by for second and third helpings of hospitality, too.

They couldn't do their jobs if they didn't love people. Or without the help of other dedicated volunteers on the bus lines like Martha Ann and Eddie Altman, Patsy Young, Nancy Murdock, Nita and Albert McLellan, Bill Causey, Mike Deep, Joe League, Ann Peake, Tena Roberts, and Roy Shults.

The Fields started as guides in 1994, with Ken narrating on the bus and Alice helping direct the driver through the city streets. They then moved to the booth, where they worked ten hours a day for eight days of the festival.

Thuente said once she booked the tour, she never had to worry about the details.

"Alice would take care of all the arrangements, from suggesting restaurants to scheduling the guides," she said. "She would work on it all year long, not just during the festival. She never forgot a tour, when they came and who they wanted for a guide. If they had not registered for the current year, she would call them and give them a special invitation. I never remember her calling me about anything. She just took care of it."

At age ninety-five, Leon "Red" Herring is the oldest festival volunteer. His official duty has been "bus dispatcher" for twenty-five of the thirty-one festivals.

"I love to meet people and mingle," he said. "I'm going to keep doing it as long as I am able."

His duties are to make sure the buses run on time. From his command post at Central City Park, he gets both the chartered buses and the Cherry Blossom Express buses rolling on the two-and-a-half-hour tour. He is there to greet them when they return. He also helps with parking and traffic flow in the park.

Herring began volunteering after festival officials approached members of the Macon Kiwanis Club about helping out. He began working with the bus tours and has never done anything else.

He sometimes gets some good-natured ribbing about his name. Growing up, nobody ever called him Leon. He had red hair, so it was a natural-born nickname. (A "red herring" is a literary device used to distract readers from a story. It was a popular expression during Harry Truman's presidency.)

Red has had shoulder surgery and a knee replacement, but that hasn't stopped him from his bus duties at the park.

Thuente lauded a host of other volunteers.

Bill Morrison, a display manager for JCPenney, was an artist who designed the backdrops for the ball and the queen and princess pageant every year. (He was a foot-note in history, too, having taught former President Bill Clinton how to play the saxophone back in Arkansas.)

Thuente said that local historian Phil Comer wrote the Cherry Blossom riding tour booklet and served as a guide himself for many years.

The Cherry Blossom Festival recognizes volunteers at a luncheon at the Macon City Auditorium. (Courtesy of Jay Jarvis)

Ernest C. Moore sold thousands of festival pins in for the Exchange Club of Macon.

Margie Hughes, Betty Hemingway, and Thelma Deep were invaluable to Thuente for the twenty years she worked at the festival. Hughes did everything from stamping letters and addressing envelopes to making judges' books. Hemingway and Deep both typed and took shorthand and did a lot of secretarial work. Thuente laughed and said they started volunteering less when computers came on the scene. But Trisha Combes started as an intern from Wesleyan and was a computer whiz who continued to volunteer with her husband, Ben.

Others worked tirelessly behind the scenes. Laverne Cantrell worked for thirty years serving ice cream in Third Street Park. Naomi Gerson was in charge of the floral decorations for the Cherry Blossom ball, and she and the Vineville Garden Club decorated for the annual volunteer awards luncheon at the City Auditorium. York Hudgins volunteered to move the decorations for the ball and the queen and princesses' decorations to and from the festival warehouse. He also delivered the brochures and schedules to all the hotels and motels in Macon.

Dale Duncan and Cynthia Smith of the Dance Center helped coordinate the Cherry Blossom Queen and Princess Pageant.

Essie Anderson was a terrific volunteer who answered the phone at the festival office. "With all lines ringing at once, Essie could answer them all and usually solve their problems and answer their questions," said Thuente. "She was willing to serve in any way."

She said that Ray and Mary Jean Hamlin and members of their Sunday school class—Sonny and Lem Redmond, Nancy, Ken and Jason Daniel, and Billy Campbell—became volunteers through their involvement with Jimmy Spires and his pink cabs in 1992.

"Ray and his crew called themselves 'Connie's Royal Guards.' They did everything from transporting VIPs from the Atlanta Airport to helping clean up after the ball," said Thuente. "One year they had a pink Cadillac convertible and drove Elvis [a look-alike] to Central City Park. You would have thought it was really 'The King' himself!"

Japanese visitors admire Yoshino trees in Third Street Park in 2002. (Photo by Beau Cabell)

BEAUTY WITHOUT BORDERS

In the cherry blossom's shade
there's no such thing
as a stranger.
—Kobayashi Issa, Japanese haiku poet

If the world wore a belt, it would be 24,901 miles around at its belly. If you took a tape measure from the top of its ice-cold head to the bottom of its frigid toes, it would cover 12,430 miles.

There are 7 continents, 196 countries, and 7 billion people. It would be impossible to reach out to all of them.

But Macon is home of the International Cherry Blossom Festival and promotes the theme of "love, beauty, and international friendship." So the city prides itself on its own kind of global outreach baptizing international visitors in blossoms, barbecue, and Southern drawls.

From the beginning, director Carolyn Crayton's mission statement was to emphasize the international component of the festival.

"I was so proud we had all this beauty and wanted to share it with the world," she said. "We wanted to make it a life-enriching experience for everybody."

The festival has helped build strong relationships with officials from Japan and Great Britain and international exchanges with dozens of countries.

It has helped promote economic ties and build friendships with Macon's sister cities in Macon, France; Kurobe, Japan; Gwacheon, South Korea; Kaohsiung, Taiwan; Elmina, Ghana; and Ulyanovsk, Russia.

"The international aspect gives us a flair others don't have," said former festival director Allen Freeman. "It shows we have built friendships and relationships with other parts of the world."

Like so many other components of the festival, the International foundation came from the Keep Macon-Bibb Beautiful Commission. Crayton's widely recognized work with Keep America Beautiful inspired her to travel to other countries. She became involved with "Clean World International," a consortium of twenty-five nations and the council of Europe that was formed to promote energy conservation and environmental preservation.

As part of its 1980 conference, the CWI sent delegates to tour three Georgia cities—Macon, Rome, and Atlanta. Georgia was the first state in the US to implement the Clean Community System (CCS), a principal program of Keep America Beautiful.

Among the officials to visit Macon were representatives from Great Britain, Australia, Canada, France, Japan, New Zealand, Bermuda, Germany, Norway, Israel, Lebanon, South Africa, Luxemburg, Sweden, and Venezuela.

A reception was held at the Macon City Auditorium, with the Girl Scouts and Boy Scouts lining the steps holding flags representing each country. Interpreters were there to assist in communication with the international visitors. At a luncheon hosted at Idle Hour Country Club, local business leader John Comer impressed the audience by addressing the visitors in fluent French.

"It opened so many doors," Crayton said. "I got to know the heads of these organizations in places like France and Japan."

She was asked to travel on behalf of Keep America Beautiful to Great Britain, which had its own "Keep Britain Tidy" campaign. She gave speeches in Wales, Ireland, England, and Scotland.

In 1983, she was invited to receive the prestigious Queen Mother's award. She met Baron Patrick Jenkin and Lord Gordon Parry of Pembrokeshire, Wales. Lord Parry, who served as chairman of Tidy Britain, was a lifelong member of the House of Lords in Wales. He was also a broadcaster and writer for television and radio and a spokesperson for mentally and physically handicapped children.

Lord Gordon Parry of Wales was a frequent visitor to the festival with a large and loyal following in Macon. (Courtesy of **Macon Telegraph**)

It was the beginning of a special friendship with Parry. He became an annual visitor to the festival and served as grand marshal of the parade in 1989. He brought fifty-five dignitaries with him that year, including the Earl of Grey and the entertainer Wyn Calvin, sometimes known as the "Clown Prince of Wales."

Parry also made arrangements for the Welsh Guard to appear at the festival.

"It was their first trip to America," Crayton said. "We had to raise the money to bring them here. But not everybody can go to London. So we were able to bring London to Macon."

Crayton and her husband, Lee, were invited guests of Queen Elizabeth II on several occasions, and she was once seated by Prince Charles.

It is fitting that Japan has had an important role in the festival from the beginning, since the beautiful Yoshino cherry trees are native to that country.

In the 1980s, there were three large Japanese companies in Macon—YKK, TKG, and Textprint. The companies donated a 3-ton decorative lantern hand-carved from solid granite by craftsmen in Kurobe, Japan, Macon's sister city. The lantern was dedicated and placed in Third Street Park at the beginning of the first festival. It was the type of decorative lantern first used in the temples of Japan, but it later began appearing in the Japanese tea gardens.

YKK was the Georgia's first Japanese-owned factory and became the top supplier of zippers in the US. The company was a major sponsor in the early years of the festival, also donating two hard-carved benches to Third Street Park. YKK financed the festival's new headquarters on Cherry Street, which opened in 1992.

Textprint and TKG were involved with making and printing the festival flags. Thousands were sold during the early years, helping the festival get started on firm financial footing.

Members of the Middle Georgia Ikebana International add some Japanese flair to the festival every year with a display of Ikebana flower arrangements at the Woodruff House on Coleman Hill, the first stop for the bus tour groups.

The Kushi Foundation, a Japanese holistic-health institute, announced in November 1999 plans to build a $20 million peace park near I-75 and Rocky Creek Road.

The 275-acre park, a gift from the organization as a symbol of "peace, hope, and international friendship" was to be called Macon International Cherry Park. The orig-

Officials at lantern in Third Street Park, a gift from Japan. (Photo by Beau Cabell)

inal plans called for an impressive 80-acre American flag designed from rows of cherry trees, an amphitheater, museum, hotel, shopping mall, and restaurant.

Michio Kushi, founder of the organization, proposed the idea to Crayton, who made one of her six trips to Japan to meet with officials there.

But the peace park never materialized.

One component of the park has remained in Macon, however. A replica of the Nike of Samothrace, the Winged Goddess of Victory, one of the most celebrated sculptures in the world, is now on display in the Georgia Sports Hall of Fame. The 2,200-year-old original is one of the top five works at the Louvre in Paris, the most visited museum in the world.

The 9-foot-tall statue weighs 1,763 pounds is made of bronze and covered with two layers of gold, and it has been appraised at $2.3 million. After plans for the park fell through, the statue was displayed at the Museum of Arts and Sciences and later moved to the Georgia Sports Hall of Fame. It is now owned by the East-West Federation in Macon.

Festival director Jake Ferro said Macon will continue its strong relationship with Japan and England during the festival. Taiwan and Russia are also important players in keeping with the theme of international friendship.

But Ferro also has a desire to include such countries as Ireland and Germany in future festivals, as well as America's neighboring countries Canada and Mexico.

"The festival is a celebration of community and a celebration of the connections we bear across the waters," said former Mercer University president Kirby Godsey. "The international friendships that have been made with people in this community have been far-reaching."

Reverend Ronald Terry, a festival board member, is pastor at New Fellowship Missionary Baptist, where both opening and closing services have been held. (Courtesy of Jay Jarvis)

AMAZINGLY GRACED

There are 1,176 Yoshinos per square mile in Macon and Bibb County, which works out to be a pretty high density of cherry blossoms.

Macon has also been hailed for having more churches per capita than any city in the country. Like the cherry trees, there are houses of worship in every pocket of the city, and in some places there is a church on every corner.

This leads to the question, is Macon the belt buckle of the Bible Belt? Do Maconites aspire to be the kind of town Mark Twain described as "not being able to throw a brick without breaking a church window"?

Of course, at least a dozen other cities have made the same claim to be first in the number of churches, including Wheaton, Illinois; Nashville, Tennessee; Pensacola, Florida; Tulsa, Oklahoma; Cincinnati, Ohio; Turlock, California; Memphis, Tennessee; Louisville, Kentucky; and two cities in Texas—Lubbock and Abilene.

Both Turlock and Pensacola have been cited by the *Guinness Book of World Records* as having the most impressive ratio of places of worship to residents. The popular board game, Trivial Pursuit, awarded the title to Wheaton, Illinois.

The churches-per-capita declaration has also been made by Las Vegas (which has the most casinos), Dallas (the most strip clubs), and Key West, Florida (the most bars).

The *New Georgia Encyclopedia* makes reference to Macon as having more churches per capita than any city in the South. According to the encyclopedia, "Clearly, religious life has been an important part of the community from its earliest years, exerting both spiritual and political influence."

In Macon, approximately 235 churches represent 43 different denominations, including some three dozen churches listed as nondenominational.

In the best-selling book *Midnight in the Garden of Good and Evil* (1994), author John Berendt wrote that in Atlanta, people ask, "What's your business?" In Augusta, they want to know your grandmother's maiden name. In Savannah, they want to know what you like to drink.

In Macon, Berendt wrote, "they ask where do you go to church."

In a city of such great faith, it should come as no surprise that there is also a religious component to the annual Cherry Blossom Festival.

Since the mid-1980s, a community worship service has been included as part of the opening weekend, and an outdoor worship service has taken place on the festival's last day. It is traditionally held in Third Street Park and is known as the "Cherry Tree Cathedral."

If there was a Genesis to this tradition, Carolyn Crayton remembers it as the day Captain Tommy Hunnicutt of the Macon Police Department stopped by her office with a suggestion. She knew him from planning security for the festival.

"He said he wanted to ask me about having a worship service," she said. "He was a member of Mabel White Baptist Church, and he wanted me to meet with pastors Jimmy Waters and Steve Johnson. I absolutely loved the idea."

The inaugural service was held on the first Sunday. A special invitation was extended to festival board members, local and state elected officials, distinguished guests, and international dignitaries—an entourage of men wearing pink sports coats and women in pink dresses, hats, shoes, and purses.

The door was open to anybody and everybody. That's what made it special. Black. White. Short. Tall. Rich. Poor. Young. Old.

Waters presided over the "Cherry Tree Cathedral" for many years. That service was started at the request of vendors from the Mulberry Street Arts and Crafts Festival, but it was open to the public and held on the festival's final Sunday at 8:00 a.m.

Waters, who died in 2004, always delivered an uplifting message and often brought members of his family to sing. He was one of Macon's best-known spiritual leaders and was a pioneer in religious broadcasting in the state, with more than 25,000 broadcasts.

Over the years, worship services have been held at other Macon churches, including Highland Hills Baptist, Vineville Methodist, Vineville Baptist, Riverside Methodist, and St. Joseph Catholic. To honor what would have been the one-hundredth birthday of William Fickling, Sr., in 2003, the service was held at his home church of Mulberry United Methodist, the mother church of all Methodist churches in Georgia.

Reverend Ronald Terry, a longtime member of the festival board, has been in the ministry more than fifty years and offered his church, New Fellowship Missionary Baptist, to host the closing day worship service. The church is just a slow roll down the hill from Fort Hawkins, the birthplace of Macon, and is located at the corner of Fellowship Avenue and Church Street, near the Macon Coliseum. Other churches that have hosted the closing worship service include Steward Chapel AME, Mount Olive Missionary Baptist, and Community Church of God.

Macon's churches have also been featured in artist Anni Moller's "Macon Houses of Worship" in 2005 and as part of the festival's activities. Mulberry Street United Methodist hosts weekday organ concerts at noon. St. Joseph Catholic Church, First Presbyterian, and Christ Episcopal Church have all been included on the festival's official tour.

And the Town and Country Garden Club once offered a walking tour of downtown's historic places of worship. It included Christ Church, the city's oldest church, established in 1825, and three other churches that opened their doors in 1826—Mulberry Methodist, First Presbyterian, and First Baptist.

Washington Avenue Presbyterian, also part of the tour, is the oldest black Presbyterian church in the state along with Temple Beth Israel and First Baptist on New Street. The cathedral-like St. Joseph's was dedicated in 1903, and its beauty is unsurpassed, with more than sixty stained-glass windows, a magnificent pipe organ, and white marble carvings, statues, and altars from quarries in Italy.

Yoshino cherry trees bloom around the Tidal Basin in Washington, DC. (Courtesy of the National Cherry Blossom Festival)

THE MORE, THE CHERRIER

Macon may have a corner on the number of blossoms, but it does not have a monopoly on the festival.

The National Cherry Blossom Festival in Washington, DC, has been around since 1935. (Yes, before there was a Tea Party, there was a Tree Party.)

The Washington festival is a two-week event, although it was expanded to five weeks in 2012 to commemorate the one-hundredth anniversary. Some say the festival might have "unofficially" begun in 1927, when a group of school children reenacted the first cherry tree planting in 1912.

The national festival takes place in April and includes parades, pageants, and concerts. An estimated 1.5 million people attend every year in celebration of spring in the nation's capital.

Macon doesn't even have exclusive rights to a Yoshino festival in Georgia. The Cherry Blossom Festival in Conyers began in 1982. It is held the final weekend in March, which means it is often going on at the same time as its big sister. The ten-day Macon festival is scheduled around William Fickling's March 23 birthday. Both festivals try to avoid Easter weekend if it falls in late March.

The crowds in Conyers are not as large, but the festival draws from the Atlanta area 30 miles away. Most of the activities are held at the Georgia International Horse Park, site of the equestrian events during the 1996 Summer Olympics.

Folks in Macon can only admire the flowering cherries, not make a meal out of them. Those who would rather eat cherries than gawk at blossoms can make the 1,034-mile journey north to Traverse City, Michigan. No need to ask for directions. All but the final 42 miles of the trip are on I-75.

The National Cherry Festival attracts about a half-million visitors every July. Yes, they munch on the cherries in Traverse City. About three-fourths of the nation's cherry crop comes from Michigan. Or, as a festival official once put it, "Macon has the blossoms. We have the pits."

The Michigan festival actually has its roots in blossoms. In the 1850s, a Presbyterian minister named Peter Dougherty planted cherry trees on the Old Mission Peninsula near Lake Michigan. The cool climate proved ideal for the cherry orchards as they began spreading across the landscape.

The festival began in Traverse City in 1926, originating from a spring ceremony known as the "Blessing of the Blossoms."

While Macon is draped in pink for its festival, the National Cherry Festival has a dark side. Its official color is dark red.

There are also annual cherry blossom festivals in Denver, San Francisco, Los Angeles, Philadelphia, Honolulu, Virginia Beach, Newark, and Pawtucket. There is a Cherry Tree Festival in Seattle and a Cherry Pie Festival in Black Hawk, Colorado.

Georgia pays homage to dozens of other trees, flowers, fruits, and vegetables. There are dogwood festivals in Perry and Atlanta. There is a pine tree festival in Swainsboro.

Flowers and blossoms are celebrated at the Forsythia Festival in Forsyth, Spring Jonquil Festival in Smyrna, Mountain Laurel Festival in Clarkesville, Geranium Festival in McDonough, Daylily Festival in Gray, Rose Festival in Thomasville, and Azalea Festivals in both Valdosta and Morrow.

The taste buds are in full bloom for festivals in Reynolds (strawberries), Fort Valley and Byron (peaches), Vidalia (onions), Juliette (fried green tomato), and Cordele (watermelons).

When it comes to festivals, the more the cherrier.

THROUGH THE YEARS

1983

The first full run of the festival received instant credibility with the arrival of NBC-TV's *Today Show* weatherman Willard Scott. Scott was greeted by a blustery morning and even a few snow flurries when he did his live report in Third Street Park. It marked the first time Macon's channel 41 (WCWB, now WMGT) had a program originated and carried live to the network. Few blossoms were around to show off to a national audience. Actress Zsa Zsa Gabor would have delivered even more of a celebrity punch, but she had to cancel her appearance. William Simmons was festival chairman. A 3-ton, 8-foot statue was unveiled in Third Street Park. It was hand-carved by craftsmen in Macon's sister city of Kurobe, Japan, and donated by local Japanese businesses YKK, Textprint, and TKG. Another gift was presented by local businessman Emmett Barnes and his wife, Edwina. The porcelain sculpture of a cherry tree branch with thirty-five blossom clusters was made at Boehm Studio in Malvern, England. It had 800 handmade pieces and took three months to make. It was later displayed at Macon City Hall. Rebecca Voyles was festival queen. Representative J. Roy Rowland secured Macon a spot in the Congressional Record as the "Cherry Blossom Capital of the World."

Macon-born actress Cassie Yates, left, of ABC's **Dynasty** was grand marshal of the parade in 1985.
(Courtesy of Cherry Blossom Festival)

1984

Vice President George Bush came to town eleven days before the festival as part of a campaign stop while running for reelection on the ticket with President Ronald Reagan. The vice president gave a fifteen-minute speech, then planted a ceremonial cherry tree in Third Street Park. Headline writers were pleased. It's not every day you have a Bush planting a tree. The tree was later moved to an undisclosed location. The blossoms were out in full force, to the delight of everyone. William Faulkner was festival chairman. For Fickling's birthday, CBS-TV sent a camera crew. The segment was aired by Charles Kuralt. Macon mayor George Israel appeared for seven seconds in the middle of seven women for a segment on ABC's *Good Morning America*. Israel took off his blue blazer and borrowed a pink sports coat. Edwina Barnes stood behind him while the cameras were on and held the jacket so that it would appear to fit. Kathy Brown was queen. Pearlie Pyles was senior queen. The *Cherries Galore* cookbook was published with 232 pages and more than 400 recipes contributed by Middle Georgians.

1985

The American Bus Association named the festival one of the "Top 100 Events in North America." Local artist Joey Pineaud designed "Macon City Limits, Cherry Blossom Capital" signs at twenty locations around the city. Blossoms were latecomers and were flashy in some parts of town and AWOL in others. Macon-born actress

Cassie Yates of ABC's *Dynasty* was grand marshal of the parade. Country singer Louise Mandrell gave a concert at the Coliseum. Borden brought in Elsie the Cow to help promote the free cherry ice cream in the park. For the first time, the festival saluted a nation, Great Britain. Mercer president R. Kirby Godsey was festival chairman. The Macon Transit Authority System announced that it would begin calling its buses "Cherry Blossom Express." Macon was named one of four national test markets for Cherry Coke during the festival, after Coca-Cola introduced the new soft drink. The other cities were Atlanta; Hartford, Connecticut; and the Charlotte/Greensboro/Winston-Salem area of North Carolina. In the past, Cherry Coke had been a favorite soda fountain concoction but had never been marketed as a product. The Cherry Blossom Commemorative Coca-Cola in a 10-ounce bottle later won for the "most innovative souvenir item" at the International Festivals and Events Association. Robin Lee was queen. Louise Young was senior queen.

Macon was a test market for Cherry Coke.
(Courtesy of Coca-Cola)

1986

The blossoms played hide-and-seek until a week after the festival, but they still managed to get national coverage on two networks' shows, *Good Morning America* and *CBS Morning News.* CBS dispatched weatherman Steve Baskerville to Macon for two live segments. The festival was named one of the top twenty events in the Southeast by the Southeast Tourism Society. Dr. Robert Ackerman, president of Wesleyan College, was festival chairman. Among the musical acts was the Four Tops. Some additional national exposure came in a wire story after one of 500 helium-filled balloons with the message "Heard School Celebrates Macon's Cherry Blossom Festival" traveled more than 1,000 miles and was found in a field near Worchester, New York. Jill Herman and Barbara Hilliard published a twenty-eight-page coloring book called "Cherry Blossom Time." Mary Therese Grabowski, who would later go on to a career in local television at WMAZ, was festival queen. Sara Landry was senior queen. Officials estimated that more than 300,000 people attended the festival, which was featured on the cover of the Macon phone book.

Mary Therese Grabowski, center, was the festival queen in 1986.
She went on to become an anchor at WMAZ-TV. (Courtesy of Macon Telegraph)

1987

The national spotlight on Macon continued with a story in *USA Today* newspaper at the beginning of the festival. It mentioned a number of the city's icons—Nu-Way Weiners, Otis Redding, Little Richard, and The Allman Brothers Band. The festival also raised a few eyebrows when it started a "blossom war" with the nation's capital over which city had the biggest and best celebration of the blossoms. To dramatize the rivalry, Macon sent army helmets to television stations in the Washington area. Dr. S. Aaron Hyatt, president of Macon Junior College, was festival president. Talk show hostess Sally Jessy Raphael filmed her TV show in front of a capacity crowd at the City Auditorium. Her topics were female wrestlers, guns, psychics, and mandatory testing for AIDS. The blossoms were wobbly out of the starting gate, despite the festival date being pushed back a week. The first annual bed race was held downtown on Cherry Street, with prizes awarded to the prettiest, ugliest, most unusual, and fastest. Shannon Caldwell was queen. Anne Beach was senior queen. A 9-inch commemorative porcelain plate, with a 24-carat gold rim, was introduced for the first time and designed by local artist Mark Ballard. Sterling Everett designed the first official Cherry Blossom

Sally Jessy Raphael visited the festival to tape her talk show at the Macon City Auditorium in 1987 and '90. (Courtesy of Cherry Blossom Festival)

painting. Greg Crawford designed the festival's official jewelry—pendants, lapel pins, and stick pins all finished in 14-carat gold.

1988

In a gesture of goodwill prior to the festival, Carolyn Crayton and Macon mayor Lee Robinson traveled to Washington, DC, to present a gift of 100 cherry trees. One tree was ceremoniously planted at the site of the Martin Luther King, Jr., time capsule on the Western Plaza. B. B. King appeared with his band in concert at the Macon Coliseum wearing a pink sports coat. The Tams performed at the popular Fifties-Sixties Dance at the City Auditorium. Former mayor Buck Melton was festival chairman. Jeff MacGregor, host of *The New Dating Game*, was grand marshal of the parade. He replaced actor Richard Dysart of NBC's *L.A. Law*, who could not attend. The Florida State High Flying Circus performed at Luther Williams Field. Melissa Dawn Shaw was queen. La Vada Allen was senior queen. Cherie, the official doll, was introduced. It was designed by Phyllis Parkins and sold for $320. It was 18 inches tall with dark brown hair, wearing a Southern belle dress of cherry blossom pink taffeta trimmed with French lace. Cherie carried an open parasol, a garland of cherry blossoms in her hair. The "real" blossoms once again played hard to get until the week after the festival, which officials said attracted about 400,000 people.

Aubrey Allen with official flag he designed.
(Courtesy of **Macon Telegraph**)

1989

The blossoms put the festival on good footing when they came out by midweek. CBS weatherman Mark McEwen appeared in the parade and broadcast live from Coleman Hill the next morning. Lord Parry brought fifty-five dignitaries in his party from England and Wales when he served as grand marshal of the parade. Princess Marie-Blanche de Brogile of Paris was a distinguished visitor. Macon's Aubrey Allen designed the festival's official pink flag. Recording artist Lee Greenwood played at the Coliseum and sang "God Bless the USA." This patriotic song, which he had performed at the 1984 Republican National Convention, would receive even greater air play in 1990 and 1991 during the Gulf War. Another song, "White Columns and Cherry Blossoms," made its debut and was written by two local women, Jackie McNair and Freda Nadler. Carr Dodson was festival chairman. Kim Young was queen. Palmira Braswell was senior queen. William David Mitchell and Haylee Melesa Lao were Little Mr. and Miss Cherry Blossom.

1990

Three-time Grammy winner Lou Rawls played to a packed house at the Coliseum during the festival. He was famous for his expression, "Yeah, buddy." After Rawls was given the key to the city, he should have added, "Yeah, buds!" The buds were out, and blossoms were peaking for most of the festival. Lionel Hampton performed at the ball. Sally Jessy Raphael was back for another show at the City Auditorium. This time, her topics were "Stars from TV Shows with a Southern Flair" and "I'm Married to a Redneck." At the close of the festival, chairman Arthur "Buster" Barry, Jr., called it the "biggest, best, and smoothest to date." Styletta Carter was queen. Inez Eddy was senior queen. John Morgan and Marquita Jenay Redd were Little Mr. and Miss Cherry Blossom. In May, the festival broke ground for its new building at the corner of Cherry and New streets, made possible by a $300,000 contribution from YKK. Officials esti-

Bibb County Schools Children's Choir rehearses for festival concert in 1991.
(Courtesy of **Macon Telegraph**)

mated that the festival took in $4.29 million. William Fickling, Sr., died in November. He was eighty-seven.

1991

The festival was featured in *Money* magazine, which cited the city's strong ties with local Japanese businesses. The blossoms showed up for a fourth-quarter rally. Former city councilman Vernon Colbert became the first black to serve as festival chairman. The musical lineup was dynamic. Ray Charles, ranked number 2 behind Aretha Franklin (and one ahead of Elvis Presley) on *Rolling Stone* magazine's "100 Greatest Performers of All Time," performed at the

The annual street party draws huge crowds to Cherry Street on final weekend of festival.
(Courtesy of Ken Krakow)

City Auditorium. Trumpeter Al Hirt and the Gatlin Brothers also gave concerts. The street party featured Chubby Checker, Three Dog Night, Jerry Reed, and the Indigo Girls. The Middle Georgia chapter of the American Institute of Architects sponsored a sand castle contest, and 100 tons of sand were dumped in Central City Park. Jennifer Chapman was queen. Beverly Gnehm was senior queen. Jay Gunter and Kristen Nichole Clements were Little Mr. and Miss Cherry Blossom. The new festival head-quarters was dedicated. The three-story, Georgian revival-style building was pink, although the festival staff described the exterior color as "blush."

1992

Comedian Bill Cosby with festival chairman Guy Eberhardt and commissioner Larry Justice. (Courtesy of Cherry Blossom Festival)

For the second straight year, the blossoms delivered at the end. Bill Cosby was a headliner with his popular comedy routine. Country music fans were pleased when Tanya Tucker and the Oak Ridge Boys played at the Coliseum. Guy Eberhardt was festival chairman. Four pink taxis from the Yellow Cab Company made their debut and appeared during Sunday's parade. "Nowhere else in the world are there pink yellow cabs," said Crayton. Jimmy Spires and his son, Ricky, agreed to paint four "yellow" cabs pink for each one of the four decades the company had served the city. They offered free rides to anyone requesting a pink taxi. The drivers wore pink shirts, hats, and ties. Kelly Jennings was queen. Sherrell Nelson Hart was senior queen. Tyler Stone and Britney Hudson were Little Mr. and Miss Cherry Blossom. The festival's first-ever Waiter-Waitress Race was held downtown. Servers from local restaurants were tested on a 40-yard obstacle course with four water-filled glasses on a tray.

1993

Tomika Miller, the Cherry Blossom queen and a student at Northeast High School, represented Macon and the festival on the "Sweet Adventure" float at the Tournament of Roses Parade on New Year's Day in Pasadena, California. Jessie Patton was senior queen. Richard McClellan and Amanda Cherlin were Little Mr. and Miss Cherry Blossom. Mickey Mouse became the first rodent to serve as grand marshal of the parade. Guy Eberhardt returned for a second year as festival chairman. Freezing temperatures were partly to blame for the poor showing of the blossoms, which did not arrive until after the festival. Overall, attendance was down. Festival officials attributed some of the drop-off to an earlier winter storm on the East Coast that caused several bus tour groups to cancel.

1994

James Brown, "The Godfather of Soul," arrived in a 38-foot limousine, complete with hot tub, to tour his old neighborhood in Pleasant Hill and to attend a ceremony to have the Walnut Street bridge that crosses I-75 named in his honor. He gave a three-hour concert at the Coliseum. It was his first concert in nineteen years in the city where he recorded his first two hit records, *Please Please Me* and *Try Me*. Another Georgian, former President Jimmy Carter, served as grand marshal of the parade. Melvin Kruger was festival chairman. The blooms were out big time, the prettiest and timeliest in years. The festival took home eleven awards from the International Festivals and Events Association convention in St. Paul, Minnesota.

Cover of the 1993 festival brochure.
(Courtesy of Cherry Blossom Festival)

There were eight gold and three silver medals—more awarded to the International Cherry Blossom Festival than to any of the other 700 festivals represented. Macon's festival had been entered in twenty of the forty-seven categories. "They weren't too heavy," said Crayton. "I had no trouble getting them home at all." Avril Cobb was queen. Mary Eva DuBose was senior queen. Tracy Aparicio Fogg and Hannah Watson were Little Mr. and Miss Cherry Blossom. Four months after the festival, Macon suffered major flooding from Tropical Storm Alberto in the worst natural disaster in state history.

1995

Blossoms were sleepyheads again and were not around for most of the festival. Al Hirt was back on his trumpet, playing beneath the copper dome of the City Auditorium, one of the largest of its kind in the world (152 feet in diameter). Country music artist Vince Gill gave a concert at the Coliseum, and .38 Special was right on target at the street party. Charles Jay was festival chairman. Kisha Demps was queen. Anne Turner was senior queen. Jovon Clark and China Grayer were Little Mr. and Miss Cherry Blossom.

Amy Pitts holds up her daughter, Abby, at Third Street Park during 2000 festival. (Photo by Beau Cabell)

1996

The unpredictable March weather was at it again. A spring freeze reduced the quality of the blossoms. Rain played havoc with the bookend weekends of the festival, canceling the Sunday parade on the opening weekend for the first time in history and putting a damper on the street party on the final Saturday. Roy Fickling, grandson of William Fickling Sr., was festival chairman. A major attraction was Gladys Knight, minus the Pips, at the Coliseum. Kelly McQuarrie was queen. Helen Smith was senior queen. Jesse Bryant Otwell and Daniele Nichole Ard were Little Mr. and Miss Cherry Blossom. The only two Georgia events publicized by American Bus Association were the Cherry Blossom Festival and the Centennial Summer Olympics in Atlanta. The association previously recognized the Cherry Blossom Festival as one of the top 100 events in North America and promoted it as a "choice designation" for motor coach tour groups.

1997

Superb weather, fantastic crowds, and perfect timing of the Yoshinos inspired Crayton to call the festival the best in its fifteen-year history. *Good Morning America* was back for three live segments from Third Street Park. Reporter Mindy Moore bantered back and forth with hosts Charles Gibson and Cynthia McFadden about the blossoms and the Macon Whoopee hockey team. As a joke, Macon police Lieutenant Danny Thigpin pulled over the *Good Morning America* motor home for making an illegal left turn. "He was like a police officer out of *Smokey and the Bandit*," Moore said, laughing. The Atlanta Rhythm Section, featuring Macon native Ronnie Hammond as lead vocalist, rocked Central City Park. Bill Forget was festival chairman. In an attempt to reach a younger, college-age audience,

The Mulberry Street Arts and Crafts Festival brings thousands downtown on the final weekend. (Photo by Beau Cabell)

eight bands were brought in for the first-ever "Cherry Palooza" at Central City Park. Eighteen "cowboys" rode a 1,800-pound Brahman bull for a shot at glory and prize money during the Cherry Blossom Rodeo. Jennifer Wall was queen. Eloise Hadaway was senior queen. Ryan Christopher Wolfe and Taylor Delane Addleton were Little Mr. and Miss Cherry Blossom. Barnes Fur, located across the corner from the festival office on Cherry Street, ordered twenty-nine Cherry Blossom Barbies with full-length pink mink coats, matching hats, genuine leather boots, and purses. The dolls sold for $125.

1998

Country star Tracy Lawrence was a big name on the marquee, and the Dixie Chicks played at the street party. A Japanese visitor from Kyoto told Crayton the Yoshino cherries were "like the ladies . . . you need to give them love and attention." Ashlee Gowder was queen. Shirley Williams was senior queen. Nicholas William Jones and Erica Rebecca Woodley were Little Mr. and Miss Cherry Blossom. A Madame Alexander doll named "Carolyn" in honor of Crayton made its debut. It was 12 inches high and was sold in a pink hatbox. One hundred fifty limited-edition dolls were sold. Dr. John O'Shaughnessey was festival chairman. The downtown trees sure could have used a little more love. They were late-bloomers again. Bill Boyd, retiring columnist of *The Telegraph*, had this to say about the festival: "You absolutely, positively cannot find a more beautiful place from mid-March to mid-April than Macon, Ga. Its people are so friendly you'll wonder why God even created crabby humans."

For many years, "Twins Day" was a popular event at Central City Park. (Courtesy of Jay Jarvis)

1999

The Macon Whoopee hockey team, with one of the greatest sports nickname of all time, switched names for a day and became the Macon Cherry Blossoms in a game against Columbus. The team wore white sweaters with pink letters and numbers with cherry blossoms. *The Washington Post* sent a reporter to explain how Macon was showing up the traditional National Cherry Blossom Festival in DC. The story claimed that for "cherry tree saturation, the Southern belle puts the Tidal Basin to shame." However, there weren't too many blossoms that year to write home about. Don Miller was festival chairman. Lauren Summers Hodgens was queen. Charlotte Lucas was senior queen. Joshua Delton Cockrell and Morgan Nichole Nichols were Little Mr. and Miss Cherry Blossom.

2000

After a wet start, a great week of weather and perfect blossoms brought out record crowds to some 500 events, including 150 musical acts. The festival included concerts by the Beach Boys, Chuck Leavell, Lonestar, and the Tommy Dorsey Orchestra. The Welsh Guard band was in the parade and gave a concert. Macon native Robert McDuffie played violin, and his sister, Margery McDuffie Whatley, gave a grand finale concert. Jantina Virgil was queen. Ester Goddard Fussell was senior queen. Brandon West and Callie Harris were Little Mr. and Miss Cherry Blossom. Fourteen members of a Friendship Force from Japan participated in the festival parade, carrying an American flag. The Cherry Palooza returned after a two-year absence. Bill Wiley was festival chairman.

2001

It was the end of an era after Crayton announced in February that 2001 would be her final festival. "In many ways, I think of the Cherry Blossom Festival as my baby," said Crayton, who would continue as a festival board member. A four-page article in the March issue of *Southern Living* magazine helped boost attendance. The blossoms jump-started and came out before the festival. They had to survive a cold blast of Canadian air two weeks prior to the first day. Macon native Little Richard gave his first concert in his hometown in eleven years at the Coliseum. He grew up on Fifth Avenue in the historic Pleasant Hill neighborhood. He brought his ten-piece band and wore an all-white suit with silver-sequined stripes. The opening act was the Atlanta Rhythm Section, which featured another hometown musician, lead singer Ronnie Hammond. There was a blues concert at Luther Williams Field, and the Perry High School marching band was selected as the festival's "honor band" after appearing in the movie *Remember the Titans*. Eddie Pruett was festival chairman. John Grinalds, president of the Citadel and a 1955 graduate of Lanier High School, was the parade grand marshal. Macon track star Antonio Pettigrew, who won an Olympic gold medal in 2000, also rode in style in the parade. Allison Gaudet was queen. Janice Hefner was senior queen. Blake Spires and Maci Smith were Little Mr. and Miss Cherry Blossom. A number of flower arrangements were on display during the "Cherished Memories" event at the Federated Garden Club's house on College Street. It featured cherry blossom, forsythia, and crabapple blossom arrangements. The festival received a full-page story in the *Christian Science Monitor*, a newspaper with a national circulation.

2002

For the first time, the festival was led by someone besides Crayton. Allen Freeman, executive director of the Georgia State Fair, was hired as director. He had experience with the festival, having spent four years as special events manager. The weather was nice, but the trees did not cooperate. Mark Stevens was festival chairman. Sabrina Sikora was queen. Betty Hines was senior queen. Chasen Reed Walston and Jordon Brooke Harrell were Little Mr. and Miss Cherry Blossom. The Band of the Welsh Guard and a dance troupe from Taiwan were among the highlights, along with New York City firefighter Lieutenant Richard Saracelli, a hero from the September 11, 2001, terrorist attack that killed 343 firefighters. Saracelli served as grand marshal of the parade and was accompanied by his wife, Gail. "You can be sure when I go back up

North to see my Yankee brothers, I'll tell them about the amazing Southern hospitality I've seen down here," he said.

2003

The patriotism of red, white, and blue joined the pink as the festival kicked off the week the US invaded Iraq. The annual volunteer awards banquet was held against the backdrop of a large American flag. The Army Grand Forces band was among the concerts during the festival. A later start to the festival (March 21) provided a good showing of blossoms for the first weekend of festivities, but they were falling stars by the week's end. The popular balloon glow was moved to the first weekend to help strengthen attendance. Sunday marked what would have been the one hundredth birthday of William Fickling, Sr., so the opening worship service was held at Mulberry Street United Methodist, his home church. Festival chairman Reverend Ronald Terry reached out to make the festival more culturally diverse, including an "Urban Night" at Central City Park. Randi Mallori Adkins was queen. Betty Sanders was senior queen. VaShaun Rozier and Michaela Woody were Little Mr. and Miss Cherry Blossom. Paschal "Pappy" English was grand marshal of the parade. English, a superior court judge from Thomaston, appeared on the CBS-TV reality show *Survivor*, making it to the final round. His daughter, Rachel English, was a former Miss Georgia and a news anchor for WMAZ-TV in Macon.

2004

Blessed with some of the best weather in years, the festival opened to a multitude of blossoms. A record crowd of 10,000 attended the balloon glow, which was moved to the Herbert Smart Airport in East Macon. Lauryn Whitfield was queen. Betty Tolbert was senior queen. Hunter Germundsen and Megan Alexis Carter were Little Mr. and Miss Cherry Blossom. The first "Cherryoke" karaoke competition was held, with festival-goers singing to recorded music. Bill Fickling III was festival chairman. After three years at the helm, Allen Freeman stepped down on April 1 at the close of one of the most successful festivals in recent history. In August, Wright Tilley, who had worked for the festival from 1992 to 1994 as director of operations, was named as the new CEO and president. In September, Lord Gordon Parry of Wales died. He was a frequent international guest and a wonderful ambassador for his friends in Macon. Dr. Bruce Allen, a festival board member, attended the funeral in Cardiff, Wales.

The International Food Fair is always a crowd-pleaser at the Mulberry Arts and Crafts Festival. (Photo by Beau Cabell)

2005

Wright Tilley began his tenure as the festival's third director. The gift shop made a move for greater visibility by leaving its location on Third Street across from the park to 577 Mulberry Street on the ground floor of the Fickling building. Eddie Pruett had a second stint as festival chairman. The "Cherry Blossom Boogie" became a revamped version of the popular Fifties-Sixties Dance. The Macon Thunder fireworks show debuted on the Ocmulgee Riverwalk. Julie Soles was queen. Gwen Peek Rayson was senior queen. Alex Bailey and Kelly White were Little Mr. and Miss Cherry Blossom. About 700 children from 30 Bibb elementary schools participated in the annual children's concert at the City Auditorium. The theme of the program was "Shoo Bop Doo Wop . . . A Cherry Blossom Hop." Wet weather forced the cancellation of several big events, including the street party. The festival also fell during Holy Week, which hurt attendance on the final weekend because of Easter. A major sponsor was lost when Brown and Williamson Tobacco, one of Bibb County's largest employers, announced the closing of its Macon plant.

2006

Chip Cherry, head of the chamber of commerce, served as festival chairman with a perfect name for those duties. The weather was blustery at the start, and chilly temperatures led to sporadic blooms all week. Said Tilley, "There was no rhyme or reason to Mother Nature this year." There was no headliner concert, although another promoter

The balloon glow is one of the biggest crowd-pleasers of the festival. (Photo by Beau Cabell)

brought in country star Kenny Rogers during the week. Macon natives Nancy Grace of CNN and Jeanetta Jones of the Weather Channel served as grand marshals of the parade. Sagen Woolery was queen. Rosetta Armour-Lightner was senior queen. Damon Rice and Hadley Michele Neal were Little Mr. and Miss Cherry Blossom.

2007

The festival celebrated its twenty-fifth year. Clydesdale horses were featured in the parade, as well as a 14-foot-high helium balloon in the shape of a birthday cake. Lowell Register was festival chairman. Former Mayor George Israel, who cut the ribbon for the inaugural festival in 1983, served as grand marshal of the parade. Brettlin Spangler was queen. Ann Simmons Davis was senior queen. Clayton Eric Fordham and Maggie May Allwein were Little Mr. and Miss Cherry Blossom. The blossoms played hard to get at the beginning of the festival but closed out strong.

2008

Trying to avoid a conflict with Easter and a repeat of 2005, the festival was pushed to a later start on March 28 and ran through April 6. It helped with the timing of the blossoms. Petals the Poodle made her debut as mascot. Linda Maddox, the event coordinator at Central City Park, launched a "Pink in the Park" to get people to "think as pink as possible." But the blooms were not on their best behavior. The weather was again wild and unpredictable. The Sunday parade on the opening weekend was windy and cold, and many of those who watched it wore coats and wrapped in blankets. Inclement weather either canceled or curtailed many of the festival's major events, including the balloon glow and air show. Rain washed out the street party, which caused the festival to lose about $120,000. Tilley departed as festival director for a tourism job in North Carolina, and board member and former county chief appraiser and tax commissioner Jim Davis agreed to serve as interim director. Shirley Buafo was festival chairman. Emily Alston was queen. Alberta Sims was senior queen. Jay Sink and Chanelle Washington were Little Mr. and Miss Cherry Blossom.

2009

There was a perfect start to the festival with sun-kissed skies, spectacular crowds, and full blossoms by midweek. Durwood "Mr. Doubletalk" Fincher was grand marshal of the parade. Fincher, who grew up in the cotton mill village of Payne City, was given a key to the city by Mayor Robert Reichert at the ball on Friday night and quipped, "Does it open the door to the Nu-Way?" Former Macon mayor Lee Robinson was festival chairman and praised Davis for filling in as interim director. "He stepped right into a void and rolled up his sleeves and got the job done," Robinson said. Governor Sonny Perdue attended the ribbon cutting for the festival with Ichiro Fujisaki, the Japanese ambassador to the United States. He was the fourth Japanese ambassador to visit Macon during the festival since its inception. Rachael Cozart was queen. Betty Ragland was senior queen. Wyatt Davis and Alaina Banks were Little Mr. and Miss Cherry Blossom. The Mulberry Street Arts and Crafts Festival was cancelled due to heavy rains on Saturday but returned with a strong day on Sunday under sunny skies.

2010

Karen Lambert, director of the Grand Opera House, took the helm. The festival opened with some international flair. There were two dozen visitors from Ulyanousk State University in Russia and nine from Macon's sister city in Macon, France. At the opening ceremony, the Russian guests accompanied a rendition of "Georgia on my Mind" on balalaikas and other Russian folk instruments. The opening weekend was very chilly, and blossoms were few. Despite the erratic weather, no events were cancelled during the festival, which got high marks. To beat the approaching bad weather at the finale, the fireworks were shot off during daylight hours, spooking several of the horses at the nearby Wesleyan College Equestrian Center. Connie Thuente, who was retiring as the senior events coordinator, was grand marshal of the parade and promised to remain involved with the festival as a volunteer. A stir was caused at the fashion show when it was announced that a drag queen would be among the participants. Steve Jukes was festival chairman. Ansley Camille Burgamy was queen. Dorothy Black was senior queen. Denzel Washington and Brayden Stokes were Little Mr. and Miss Cherry Blossom. Lambert reported in May that the festival had turned a profit of more than $130,000.

2011

The opening and closing weekends provided a sharp contrast. The festival started under near-perfect weather conditions and ended with heavy storms, forcing cancellation of the street party and several final-day activities. The opening ceremony provided a moment of silence following a devastating earthquake and tsunami in Japan the week before the festival. Kareem Jackson, an NFL player with the Houston Texans who had played at Macon's Westside High School, was the parade's grand marshal. The balloon glow changed its name to Tunes and Balloons and continued to have success at its new venue, Macon State College. Thomas Wicker was festival chairman. Madison Mitchell was queen. Jan Thiese was senior queen. Selton Farrar and Jane Martin were Little Mr. and Miss Cherry Blossom.

2012

Karen Lambert announced that she would leave her position after the festival, the fifth change in leadership in the past decade. Steve Farr was festival chairman. Barbara Eden, star of the classic comedy *I Dream of Jeannie*, came to Macon as a special guest of the 2012 festival and grand marshal of the parade. "This is my first time in Macon but not in Georgia," she said. "The people are friendly and warm and very pink, which happens to be my favorite color." (She chose pink as the primary color of the genie costume that made her a national and international television star. The costume is now in the archives of the Smithsonian.) Festival board member Thomas Wicker called it one of the best festivals ever. "The cherry blossoms bloomed right on time; the weather was perfect. Everything turned out well. The parade was one of the best attended I've ever seen." Abigail Jones was queen. Sheila Barnes was senior queen. Tyler Burnett and Faith Buice were Little Mr. and Miss Cherry Blossom. Lambert said that visitors from

Elton John wore a pink jacket for his 2013 concert at the Macon Coliseum. (Photo by Beau Cabell)

several different countries were represented during the festival, including Israel, Japan, Canada, Cuba, Taiwan, Great Britain, Australia, Saudi Arabia, and Austria.

2013

Jake Ferro, who had been interim director, was named to the permanent position just two weeks before the festival. Crowds were great during the first weekend, but rain played havoc the rest of the way. Festival-goers spent a fair amount of time dodging raindrops and cool temperatures. Some Third Street Park festivities during the week had to be moved to the Terminal Station. The street party on the final weekend was shifted to the City Auditorium, and the Mulberry Street Arts and Crafts Festival moved to the State Farmer's Market. Central City Park events were washed out the final weekend, but officials called the festival an overall success. Elton John sold out the Coliseum and wore a pink jacket. Cyndee Busbee was festival chairwoman. Hannah Moore was queen. Shirley May was senior queen. Holden Wimberly and Remie Heidi were Little Mr. and Miss Cherry Blossom.

Festival director Jake Ferro and his wife, Michele, walk the runway at the festival's fashion show in 2013. (Photo by Beau Cabell)

BACK TO THE FUTURE

Jake Ferro is accustomed to making sports analogies and using the lessons learned on the playing field as metaphors for life.

After all, he was a star linebacker at Youngstown State in Ohio. He was drafted by the Miami Dolphins in 1967, who selected him in the fifteenth round after taking quarterback Bob Griese with their number one pick.

When he took over as president and CEO of the Cherry Blossom Festival in November 2012, just five months before the start of the 2013 festival, Ferro looked at the scoreboard and vowed to stay in the game.

Festival CEO Richard Brewer left after just four months on the job, and two staff members departed before the festival began.

"It's almost like you're down 30-0 at halftime, and you come out in the third quarter and try to stay in the game until you get your game plan going," he said.

Ferro grabbed the reins as interim director, then was offered the position full-time in February, less than a month before the start of the festival. His strong business background provided the perfect fit. He came to Macon in the mid-1980s and was president of J. M. Huber's kaolin clay division. He also served as president and CEO of Bonsal American in Charlotte, North Carlina, a leading manufacturer of packaged building materials and pavement maintenance products.

Against long odds, the 2013 festival was able to cross the finish line. The weather once again played havoc with many of the outdoor events, and the blossoms didn't fully cooperate until after the festival ended. But Ferro and his staff used it as a learning experience.

They spent much of the off season looking at the big picture, going forward with what worked and analyzing the aspects of the festival that needed improvement. Through the festival exchange program, he attended other festivals in Minneapolis and San Antonio.

"Our festival is a monumental event that has a ripple effect throughout the state, with a $10-15 million economic impact on Middle Georgia," he said.

The challenge is to blend new ideas with time-tested ones. The festival has a slate of traditional events people know and love. They provide backbone.

But the festival cannot afford to stand still and rest on its laurels. Ferro is open to tweaks and even wholesale changes. He knows that "success" comes before "work" only in the dictionary.

He remembers a Liberace concert he attended in Indiana a few years back. The flamboyant piano player and entertainer performed in front of a packed house, and Ferro had seats on the third row.

"The show was phenomenal," Ferro said. "He came out at the intermission to thank the crowd and answer a few questions. A young man asked him if he was so great, why did he need to practice? Liberace told him he practiced four hours every day. If he didn't, he would go in the opposite direction. You have to keep your edge."

One way the festival office can keep its edge is to maintain stability on the staff and to grow sponsorships, Ferro said. Among the new approaches being tried for 2014 and beyond is an extended week of activities after the festival, with an emphasis on community service.

"We always do a lot of pre-festival events like the pageant, the art reception, and the Think Pink celebration," Ferro said. "We are planning a number of events after the festival that will tie in with National Volunteer Week and to work with organizations around town to have a community outreach week."

Ferro is determined to keep the festival grounded while also leading it to new heights.

"People love to talk about the Cherry Blossom Festival," he said. "It makes people proud. Our purpose is to make it grow."

ACKNOWLEDGMENTS

I would like to thank my employer, *The Telegraph* in Macon, Georgia, for its support and assistance with this project. Newspapers are history books that write themselves every day. I could not have researched these pages without the legwork of dozens of writers, editors, photographers, and graphic artists over the past thirty-one years.

A special thanks to veteran photographer Beau Cabell, who has provided a body of his fine work. Beau has probably taken more pictures of Cherry Blossom events than anyone who has ever looked through a camera lens. I appreciate his enthusiasm and cooperation in making this book come to life.

Harriet Comer, our newspaper's librarian for many years, was a tremendous resource and help, as she has been with my other books. Harriet has a deep love of her community and its history. She is a Macon treasure.

My former publisher, George McCanless, first approached me about writing the book in August 2012. George is now the president and CEO of the United Way of Central Georgia and will serve as the Cherry Blossom Festival chairman for 2014.

I spent many hours in the homes of two gracious women, Connie Thuente and Carolyn Crayton, interviewing them and discussing the history of the festival. No one is more passionate about the Cherry Blossom Festival than these two ladies. Their institutional knowledge was invaluable. Also, many thanks to current director Jake Ferro and his staff. The festival is in good hands for years to come.

A heartfelt appreciation to Bill Fickling III for all the information and stories he provided and for being a proud and devoted spokesman for his family.

And, finally, hugs and kisses to my family for being so supportive. They know, better than anyone else, why I attach a quote at the end of all my e-mails: "Being a writer is like having homework every night for the rest of your life."

INDEX